Happiness Calling

A Practical Guide for Saying Yes to Life's Joy

By Victoria L. Mitchell, RN, LCSW

Victoria L. Mitchell

NORTHAMPTON HOUSE PRESS

Acknowledgment is made for kind permission to reprint the following:
Excerpts from *A Return to Love* by Marianne Williamson. © 1992. Reprinted by Permission of Harper Collins Publishers.
Excerpts from *Velveteen Rabbit, The Classic Edition* by Margery Williams Bianco. © 1974. Reprinted by permission of Cider Mill Press.
First edition by Northampton House Press. Cover by Naia Poyer.
ISBN 978-1-937997-87-8
Library of Congress Control Number: 2018931826

10 9 8 7 6 5 4 3 2

*This book is dedicated to my husband, who is my heart,
to my family members, who are my soul,
And to my clients, who allowed me to be
a companion on their journeys.*

Ever since Happiness heard your name,
It has been running through the streets
Trying to find you.
And several times in the last week,
God Himself has come to my door—
So sweetly asking for your address,
Wanting the beautiful warmth of your heart's fire.

—- Hafiz of Persia

Contents

Preface

A natural born therapist–that's me. Allow me to provide context for that statement, and introduce myself.

I discovered my gift for listening and mediating early, as I buffered my teenaged parents' passionate temperaments. Like most of us, they were good people doing the best they could with what they'd been given. We grew up together, with me being the steadying force in the storms.

My childhood and teen years developed many sides of this gift: problem-solver, girl next door, sympathetic ear for friends, and shoulder to lean on. In college, I advanced to listening to young men cry in their beer, a fair share of codependent rescues, and being the go-to person if someone needed bail money or a middle-of-the-night ride.

But during college, it seemed to be just a personality trait. As an English major, I would write the great novel one day. That took center stage in my dreams. Fancying myself an intellectual and political activist, I frequented coffee houses, debating the great poets and solutions to the Vietnam War.

The turbulent Sixties, decade of peace, love, and rage, formed the great divide for many women. On one side was college . . . a place to find a husband and a "just in case" career. On the other side was college . . . a vehicle for women to become corporate players, as well as wives and mothers—or not. Dangling between the Fifties and the Seventies, I chose the safe road, leaving lofty goals unpursued in favor of an ill-fated marriage.

Seven years later, that codependent union dissolved. I'd not stayed in school long enough to qualify for the "just in case" career. Random jobs led me to nursing school. The attraction to a helping profession may have been inevitable, considering my need to caretake and rescue. With an intensive-care-unit job secured, and a valedictorian award guaranteed, I began the last semester's clinical rotation–mental health.

It was like coming home. I've never left.

For the next eight years, I worked as a second shift nurse on a forty-six bed in-patient unit. Every therapist should spend time with the acutely mentally ill. It's an opportunity to witness the human spirit's capacity to adapt and survive. These intelligent and sensitive individuals taught me so much. In the throes of psychosis, some spent time as Ronald McDonald or Jesus, but none ever lost the ability to teach me great truths. Gentle souls transitioned to violent cowpokes, refined ladies to burlesque stars, and shy teens to head-banging musicians. If I was willing to follow the trail, their transformations made a mystical sense. When a patient's mind cleared and he or she was firmly grounded in reality once more, we would say our goodbyes, both knowing we might meet again in a few weeks or months. Life's crises were landmines for their fragile spirits, often necessitating another visit.

Those eight years confirmed that mental health was my career destiny. Instead of furthering my nursing education, I finished the bachelor's degree, started so long ago at Bradley University, but in psychology, rather than English. For three years, life consisted of school and work with little time for anything else.

But priorities change. Beginning my own therapy helped me recognize the intensity of inpatient work and its toll on my heart. A new marriage and my first child's birth created a different lifestyle. Inpatient mental health work had given me years of professional experience and reward, but it was time to focus on employment more compatible with raising a family.

That pursuit led me to the next thirty years as a psychotherapist, first in a psychiatric group and later in a psychologist-based practice. I was honored to work with clients in these less acute outpatient settings, embarking on many journeys of the healing heart.

Initially, this transition carried its own challenges. It was difficult to let clients with some level of risk walk out of my office. There'd been security at the hospital. I'd tucked everybody in at night and watched over them. It took time, and my own continued work, to get to a place of comfort.

I continued my education, pursuing a master's degree in social work at the University of Illinois. When graduation day finally arrived, my entire family, including three children, sat in the front row.

My licensure to practice is as a Licensed Clinical Social Worker. I also maintained my registered nursing license–these making up the letters you see after my name: RN, LCSW.

As a therapist, I found opportunities to appear on local television and radio programs to comment on newsworthy mental health issues. There were a few years of teaching psychology and social work courses at a junior college. And I had time to write articles on relevant topics. I enjoyed contributing op-eds to local newspapers and essays to regional magazines. I became a writer after all, and discovered one may not need to write the Great Novel to make a contribution.

Years of refining my skills led to multiple specialties, working with adults, couples, and groups. My expertise ranged from anxiety, depression, and relationship issues to divorce, life transitions, court mediation, and wellness. My nursing background gave me the opportunity to work with chronically and terminally ill clients. As a provider for Medicare, I worked with the senior population, who often felt more comfortable seeing a professional with an R.N. after her name.

My life has brought its share of pain and grief. Part of going on after loss is making some good come from the sorrow. My healing led to a focus on grief work, sharing many loss journeys with hurting clients. Loss also gave me an insight into reproductive grief issues—infertility, miscarriage, stillbirth, neonatal loss, and abortion.

A therapist never stops learning, whether it be through his or her own life experience or the programs and training required to maintain licensure. We never stand still in our efforts to keep up with changes in the field. We also learn from each client who enters our office. I'll share much of what I learned with you here in this study of the pursuit of happiness.

I've now begun the next phase of my journey, adjusting to retirement. I don't practice anymore. This book is not intended to be therapy. My goal is that it be a resource for personal learning and exploration.

Anecdotes, case references, and examples used in this volume are a compilation of my experiences and those of others, as well as a modest degree of creative license. Proper names and some identifying details have been changed to protect the privacy of individuals.

This book does not provide psychological services, and I am not acting in a professional capacity. I've included advice about how to find a therapist, should you choose to seek professional help.

Throughout the text, I offer theories and thoughts about the topic of happiness. Some are based on solid research, and for those, I provide references. Others come from the biases and beliefs of a stubborn, opinionated therapist, forged over the decades. My former colleagues and employers may not always agree with these, but they have served me and my clients well.

I hope you'll find these anecdotes, examples, illustrations, and exercises informative and entertaining, as well as meaningful and useful, and that this book helps you find happiness at every turn.

HAPPINESS CALLING

6

<u>Part I</u>

Chapter 1:
What You Seek is Looking for You

Happiness likes to have its way with us. It hunts us down and haunts our shadows, teasing us with many flirting faces. There are near misses and deep dives into joy.

Happiness arrives in smells and sights and sounds. It hides in new car leather, a puppy's fur, rain on a tin roof, or a sunrise. It floats there waiting for someone to notice, eager to trigger a lingering smile.

Like infatuation, happiness dangles itself before us. It courts us with flowers and dizzying moonlight. We succumb to its charms, thinking this time it will last forever, only to discover it wasn't looking for a long term commitment. It's a fling. The glow wanes, and the glitter flakes off our clothes and eyelashes.

But it gives a glimpse of the rush and flush of "perfect" happiness. You know, the constant feel good promised by seductive cultural stimuli? Advertisers assure us their products will make happiness last. We feel like a failure if the right body, partner, or job doesn't produce perpetual joy. There's the chronic temptation to follow the enticements and become immersed in the accumulation of *stuff—magic* stuff that will make us happy forever.

The brief encounters tease us into believing. Then we're left disillusioned as the flirtation wanes, lamenting that happiness never lasts. We're not meant to be happy. It's for others. Not us. The societal fantasy of constantly feeling good brought many people to my office, as they wondered what was wrong with them. After journeys of exploration, we found the absence of happiness wasn't the culprit. It was the inability to see it, flirt with it, grasp it, and be grateful it had its way with us.

The number one task is not to find happiness, but to get out of our own way and let it find us. Only then, when we allow the bursts of joy to be what they are, can we embrace the fleeting flashes that delight us along the way.

In wanting it to last forever, we miss the moments of bliss that create life's rhythm. Don't discount ecstatic moments just because they're fleeting. They warm our heart and flush our cheeks, leaving a sweet taste on the tongue and a lifetime of memories. Bursts of joy are like spindly twigs and red pine brush lit beneath sturdy logs. Tiny sparks gather strength, slowly building into something substantial and meaningful.

Each of us is unique, but we all seek joy. Its quest is a universal thread that connects us. And why shouldn't it? It's a biological preset. We come wired for happiness. Brain signals trigger chemicals that create feelings of contentment and glee. The senses stand at the ready for these shots of bliss.

We're wired for joy, but not promised a constant flow. We are, however, guaranteed ups and downs with a regular dose of troubles and trials. It's our job to find meaning in the trials and catch happiness as it flits by.

In accepting happy moments as impermanent gifts, we open ourselves to a lasting, quiet peace. If we appreciate each spark of the fire, it creates a contentment that warms us amid life's storms.

Ralph Waldo Emerson wrote, "The purpose of life is not to be happy. It is to be useful, to be honorable, to be compassionate, and to have it make some difference that you have lived and lived well."[1] The irony is that these are also the sturdy, long-burning logs of lasting contentment.

If we shift our focus to living a good life and making our days count for something, it builds lasting, soul-contented satisfaction. This is the happiness waiting for you: both fleeting glee and steadfast peace.

I offer my experience as a guide for your quest.

Chapter 2:
Beginnings

I relaxed in my faded office chair, lulled by the slowly shifting shadows of the afternoon sun, and reflected on my career. While packing retirement boxes, I sorted through gifts, treasures, and cards from clients tucked between books and photos. Years of memories brought smiles and tears.

These memories from that last day in my office were the seed of this book. My initial intention was to share topics that came up frequently with clients throughout my career. But it's also evolved into a memoir of sorts as I realized how my personal experiences nurtured my therapy skills. These imparted richness and depth as I learned how to get out of my own way.

Times of stumbles and crumbles led to my own therapy. While I learned much through studies and experience, a great deal was also given by grace. I offer you this unique perspective for what you can make of it and take from it.

Everyone is on a path of growth, whether it unfolds at the kitchen table, on the street, or in a counselor's office. I want to demystify anything in your mind and heart that might need dealing with. Some pages will seem written just for you. Your task is to honor what you carry, giving it the attention it deserves. Seek the nuggets you find meaningful. Take notes. Draw pictures. This is your book, your path, and your life.

You won't find a lot of formalistic research or theorizing. This is a volume of lessons and experience gleaned from a fruitful career. I believe in uniqueness, quirkiness, and freedom of spirit in a world that seeks sameness. We're all just human beings, doing the best we can with what we've been given.

My years of work with clients held sorrow and pain, but also laughter. The office was a haven for feelings . . . all kinds of feelings. It was a safe place to kick and scream, but also in which to laugh with abandon and experience the freedom of unrestrained joy. Each path of healing was unique. None of us knew where it would lead. We uncovered mysteries together, not knowing when moments of freedom would come.

I counted the gifts of the journey as my clients', but also as my own. I now share these gifts with you, a compilation of puzzle pieces falling into some order as we tackle the mystery of happiness.

Years with clients hung a rich tapestry in that office. The threads are woven throughout these pages as we look at how early learning and childhood experiences can block us from hearing the call of happiness. After exploring the obstacles, we'll look at gateways to growth—the art of self-care and the practice of mindfulness. Finally, we'll address general truths about common topics, and create a toolbox to take along on your happiness quest.

You'll find exercises scattered throughout the book. I encourage you to complete them.

Happiness is looking for you. Can you hear it call your name?

Chapter 3:
What Blocks Your View of Happiness?

This section addresses the emotional baggage we carry and the unhealthy coping skills it creates. These skills are like old shoes–smelly, worn-out, and worn-down. Cracks let in rain and broken soles cause pain. But they're oh so comfy in a pinching, squeaking sort of way. These scruffy shoes become a part of us. We'll miss them when they're gone.

That is, until we get a new pair. At first those are stiff and don't feel right on our feet. But once they're broken in, we see what a drag the old shoes really were. We can't imagine ever putting them on again.

Like the old shoes, some childhood coping skills are worn out and no longer helpful. These skills came from early life experiences. Even though we've outgrown them, we want to hold on. They may have kept us safe in an unsafe world. That fact alone makes it hard to just move on. These coping skills we developed as children served us well, especially in cases of trauma. As adults, they get in the way and keep us from seeing happiness.

Let's go shopping. A little retail therapy! We're looking for the shoebox labeled *Better Fit–Adult Size*. This box contains new life management skills and coping techniques. At first, nothing will feel as comfortable as those early methods. We won't want to let go. But let's seize the tethers of childhood that hold us down, and throw them away. We'll soon be ready to try new ways of dealing with challenges, and grasp those sparks of joy.

The tethers of old coping skills can take many shapes. Sometimes, it's chaos in our lives that holds us back. A few examples:
-toxic relationships
-self-sabotage
-recurrent trauma
-chronic disappointment
-workaholic habits
-procrastination and avoidance.

These old tethers can manifest in our lives in many ways:
-anxiety
-depression
-chronic stress
-social isolation
-addiction
-physical symptoms.

Whatever form they take, they hold us back from happiness. They reflect our self-view in relation to others and the world in which we live. These old habits may brand you with low self-esteem and pervasive feelings of not being lovable, or worthy of good things. The devil of negativity may whisper, "Why bother? You're not worth it." Let's quiet any of those whispers in order to take control and hear happiness instead.

To begin this journey of understanding, it's important to get to know who you were as a child. That small version of yourself still lives within you. Honoring and loving this inner child is a primary step to freedom. The first steps in nurturing this valuable relationship are found in Exercise 1.

Exercise 1: The first task is to create a timeline of your life history. You can do this over several days or in one sitting. This exercise will give you a visual reference of where you come from. In telling your story, you're able to better understand your history, and look at the life events that made you who you are. It will help you, also, gain perspective on your journey and see the whole picture.

You'll need a pencil, loose-leaf paper, and tape. You may also want to add colored pencils, markers, and stickers. Tape several sheets of the loose-leaf paper together horizontally, end to end. Use more paper than you think you'll need. You'll surprise yourself with how much you recall!

Draw a horizontal line across all the sheets somewhere near the middle. Write your life events on top of the horizontal line. First, place general life markers such as birth, schools, moves, and siblings. Then go to your more personal memories. If there was trauma or loss, or momentous happy times, put them down at the appropriate age. As you continue, more memories may come. Put them all down. You may also discover periods of your life where you can recall few memories. Note these times in parentheses. They can be as revealing as the vivid memories.

Now sit back and look at your work. You'll find feelings come as you document and study your life events. Note these emotions on your timeline under the triggering event below the horizontal line. This connects the feeling to the memory, both on the timeline and in your heart.

Take a minute for the feelings that come up. Honor what's there.

***

When you've finished looking over your work, neatly fold all the papers together. You will go back to it later. Put the timeline in your special stuff drawer. If you don't have a special place for your treasures, now's the time to create one. Just having that space helps you feel a little more special.

Your timeline is a living document. Return to it and make additions as memories and feelings arise. It can be basic or as creative as you like, incorporating illustrations and art. It's a map of your journey. Think of it as the introductory text to the story of you, and how you fell in love with your inner child.

As you create your timeline, pay attention to dreams. Sometimes new memories or feelings sneak in via the unconscious, before peeking over the horizon to conscious thought. At first these dreams might not make sense, but they'll provide clues.

One of my clients denied she had problems with trust. Then she had a dream about her best friend, her most trusted person. In the dream, her friend led her down a long, winding tunnel. She followed without question. At the end of the twisting journey, in a cold, dark cave, her friend turned around and shot her.

She trembled and sobbed as she recounted this unconscious journey. While troubling, this dream was also emotionally revealing. It opened a window to her fear and vulnerability. It gave her feelings and words that initiated her work on learning to trust.

While I was working with clients, obstacles took on a life of their own. We often named them, for the sake of illustration. These names became a therapy lingo between us. I use these phrases, now, to identify what can hold us down from flight.

In understanding what keeps us stuck, we learn the secret of breaking free.

Chapter 4:
Caution: Child on Board

Robert Fulghum wrote a book titled *All I Really Need to Know I Learned in Kindergarten*. A more accurate, but perhaps less wry, title might be, *Everything that shapes my world view, I learned by kindergarten*. We discovered our sense of place, and almost everything about feeling safe and lovable, by age six. We determined whether this world was loving and gentle or not. If it felt frightening and unsafe, we developed skills that kept us emotionally protected. The conflict lies in how these effective skills of youth follow us to adulthood, where they can become barriers to emotional freedom, limiting our capacity for intimacy and connectedness.

You may or may not have experienced childhood trauma. Still, you probably carry baggage. We all have hurtful, sorrowful memories. If you're fortunate, they were balanced by a nurturing, loving family. It's important to honor that, but it's also essential to deal with hurts. As you look at early wounds, you may feel guilty or disloyal by thinking about the people who hurt you. You defend them and say they aren't to blame. But this isn't about blame. It's about understanding.

An early loss, traumatic family event, or moment of shame may still cling to your heart. Your story includes anyone who let you down, hurt you, or disappointed you. Your quest is for knowledge, awareness, and validation.

Touching these scars from childhood can hurt. Shrapnel from your youth may be stuck in your shoulder, or throat, or soul. If you're reluctant to reflect on the shortcomings of people who matter to your story, it may be the result of a niggling voice of childhood tightening your belly. It might be telling you to be quiet because you were told to keep secrets when you were young. You say, "I love them. They did the best they could." This buries your sorrow along with the memory. The incongruity of that denial is a trap. Acknowledgment of the hurt sets you free. The goal is to understand *why* you feel the way you feel.

Remember, again, this isn't about blame, but about understanding. They really did do the best they could. But you can't honor that child you were by denying your hurt or shame now. As an adult, you're free to break the rules imposed on you as a child. Giving yourself permission to do that is the secret to a healthy adulthood, in spite of a troubled childhood.

Some childhood wounds are major, but most of us also recall little hurts and embarrassments. We all have shaming moments of forgetting the lines of a poem, a basket or goal we mistakenly made for the opposing team, the first grade pants-wetting, a class party to which Mom forgot to bring the treats, or the missing invitation to a classmate's birthday.

One of my clients spent her childhood struggling with threatened abandonment by an emotionally scarred mother. This left her particularly vulnerable to what she considered "silly embarrassments." She spent a lot of time lamenting that she was too sensitive. Yet she still carried her eight-year-old self's memory of a Sunday-school teacher's criticism of her first piano accompaniment—in front of the whole school. To this day, she continues to dislike "What a Friend We Have in Jesus."

Another embarrassing and hurtful moment occurred in first grade when she began wearing thick glasses. On the way to lunch one autumn afternoon, a high school senior, named Roseanne, laughed at her and called her "four eyes." She still remembered the midday sun's glowing, golden aura around Roseanne's head—and the burning of her flushed, little girl cheeks.

Then came the retirement of her favorite fifth grade teacher. She wrote her a poem. The music teacher praised it and asked to use it at a retirement tea. My client felt proud and was excited to read it at the tea. Then came the word someone else would actually deliver the poem—her friend with long blond hair, blue eyes, and freckles, who looked a little like Alice in Wonderland. My client, with the thick glasses and mousy brown hair that wouldn't hold curls, wasn't even given credit in the program for writing it.

By telling her stories, she validated her feelings of hurt and rejection. She was also able to name these events for the first time, as thoughtless acts by adults. It freed her of the inner voice insisting it was nothing and that she was being too sensitive. In tracing the hurt, she was able to let go of shame. She was able to forgive.

No matter your story, the lessons you learned when you were small taught you whom to trust, when to be quiet, and when not to cry. These lessons were the earliest messages about your self-worth. It can be tough growing up even in the strongest family system. You survived, as did my client. But she learned she trusted only her daddy with her piano skills, that she was worthy of ridicule in her glasses, and that looks outweighed talent.

What did you learn?

You may think they're little things. But we each have a cache of hurts tucked near our heart that impact how we feel about ourself. Acknowledging these, and the attendant feelings they carry, validates the child we were and the adult we've become.

Maybe you were the shy first grader who cried each morning when your mom left you at the school door. There might have been a physical difference that marked you, keeping you outside the playground circle. You may have been the small child, or the poor child, who was victim to bullying. Or you may have been that bully, who was a victim at home. Maybe yours was a family of high achievers, and you came up short. Or you shared life with a trouble-causing sibling, and you, the good kid, were eclipsed on his stage.

If small hurts teach us such significant lessons, what about someone who survived a childhood of trauma or abuse? First, in honoring the child you were, it's important to see the value of the skills that were honed for survival.

I used to facilitate Adult Children of Alcoholics (ACOA) groups. The silent mantra of a child growing up in an alcoholic home was, "Don't talk. Don't trust. Don't feel." This shaped the early learning of those born into these and other chaotic families. That learning signaled when to keep quiet and what secrets to hold. There was danger in thinking outside of what they were told.

During this early developmental phase, children born into more functional families learn about boundaries. Healthy parenting provides needed structure. Consistent patterns and limits develop a sense of place—a sense of safety. A few tantrums and power struggles may be spawned along the way, but children emerge on the other side feeling loved and secure.

The children born into chaos missed this valuable emotional groundwork. The unpredictability of their parents' behavior forced them to develop an alternative set of skills—without a safety net of boundary or reliability. Such children learned to read the mood of the room as preschoolers. They were baptized into the art of hypervigilance, alert for the first hint of possible threat. This early warning system was imbedded in the neural pathways of the brain, keeping them forever hyperalert for impending trouble.

They didn't trust people, and for a good reason. The parents they looked to for safety were not trustworthy. No wonder they kept their mouths shut. They never knew what would happen if they said the wrong thing, so they said nothing. They always felt "fine" for a good reason. Emotional numbness had its function too. The coping mechanisms of "Don't talk. Don't trust. Don't feel," served them well. They learned to monitor moods and to get out of the way before trouble started. These skills were valuable. They helped those born into chaos become survivors.

But just as we outgrow dolls, action figures, and old shoes, we also outgrow the need for these coping skills. What worked as a child gets in the way of trusting and authentic adult relationships, where we're expected to share feelings and rely on each other. And trust. And talk. And feel. And love.

That was then. This is now. Children like these were victims of a toxic environment. You may have been one of them. It's time to honor that little boy who shuddered behind the door or the tiny girl who sobbed as her stuffed animal was flung into the rain. Grieve for the preschooler who bandaged a puppy's bleeding paws, another victim of a family dinner gone bad. Cry for the eight-year-old who lived on the potato chips delivered along with Mommy's vodka. What would you expect these wounded souls to do? These babies were busy with the business of surviving, numbing feelings, and sharpening the early warning system.

The first step to freedom is honoring that small child. We all need to love and cherish who we were before we can love and honor our adult self. Getting in touch with this child and grieving a lost childhood is a journey as challenging as learning to walk again after months with a leg in a cast.

In the next exercise, we continue the focus on your child and his or her role in your life. At first you might feel silly dwelling so much on your childhood self. We generally don't spend much time talking about that as adults. We tend to discount the most formative years of life. We say, "That was when I was just a kid," or "Before I grew up." It's okay to go back there anyway.

***

Exercise 2: The purpose of this exercise is to help you develop a sense of softness for the child you were, the child born with shiny eyes and innocent dreams.

Take your timeline out of your special stuff drawer and look at your first six to ten years. Get a few more sheets of paper and sketch yourself in the midst of some events you remember. Stick people are allowed. So are yellow sunshine circles with rays spoking out, or angry-faced clouds with rain dots falling down overhead.

Think about the child you're drawing. What made you happy? What made you laugh? Who and what did you love? Who did you feel safest with? Think about holiday memories. Sit with the feelings you experience during this exercise. See where they take you. You may find tears welling up . . . maybe tears you've never allowed yourself to shed.

***

This assignment begins to soften your heart toward your child. Carry that gentler, more vulnerable heart with you as you progress through your journey.

With this gentle heart, you will begin to see that each childhood hurt chipped away at your sense of being okay. As a small child, you didn't have the insight to understand Daddy was a drunk, or Mommy was insecure and needy. They were your parents, so they must have been right. In your sweet little heart, whatever went wrong at your house was directly related to something you did.

Until about school age, we have an egocentric view of self in relation to the world. Anything that happens comes from us. It's a developmental task to eventually understand that we're not the center of the universe. But circumstances aren't always conducive to this realization.

In a home filled with chaos, you learned that bad things happened at your house, and it must be something you did wrong that caused it. If anything was ever going to be ok, *you* had to fix it. *You* had to be good, or better, or quieter, or prettier, or whatever. But the harder you tried, the more helpless and ashamed you felt.

In reality, you had no control over your family members' behavior, and since the problems were not really due to you but to them, you inevitably failed. This inability to change things led to the first negative feelings about yourself and the birth of your shame. Yet you kept trying:

"If I could just be quieter, my family would be okay."

"If I were just good enough, Mommy and Daddy would love me."

"If I could stop being bad, they wouldn't get so mad and fight."

"If I could just fix what was wrong with me. . . . "

"If I could be perfect. . . . "

These reactions were the beginnings of feeling unlovable and trying desperately to find some way to be loved, to be okay. If that meant, "Don't talk. Don't trust. Don't feel," so be it.

Once you get to know your child better, you'll develop a loving relationship. A new gentleness will tug at your heart. You'll begin to understand the need to love and honor your little surviving hero. You'll start to appreciate who you are, and why some things are hard. You'll learn to respect the challenge of letting go, and begin to try a smidgeon of trust.

This is the dawning of awareness of how you and your child worked together all these years. You will continue to do so. Only now, you the adult, will be in the driver's seat.

As adults we are no longer victims of our childhood or those who once victimized us. We get to choose the quality of life we want. We do the work to break free of those tethers. A big part of that task is accepting this sweet child, embracing her, and honoring her for how very hard she worked. By doing this we gain the control, and get to make the choices that define our adult life.

***

Exercise 3: Take nice, even, deep breaths, and close your eyes for a brief mental imagery exercise. Imagine your inner child sitting beside you. Hug that little one with love and tenderness. Your child has some keys clenched tightly in his fist. Tell him it's okay to give you the keys. You'll drive. Promise to keep him safe. Tell him it's going to be all right. He can trust you. You're taking him to the next stage of the journey.

Now open your eyes, but still feel the hug—and the keys in your hand.

***

As this process of embracing our child bears fruit, we become aware of how maintaining old coping skills colors our

24

perceptions. We see that we've been viewing the world through a childhood filter. As an adult, this can leave us mistrustful and wary, sensitive to criticism, and fearful of social situations. There will be many unnecessary challenges in our relationships if we remain self-protective and defensive. Seen through the filters of a broken childhood, the world remains unsafe. Danger lurks.

The eyes of the adult see more clearly. We realize the need to be open and vulnerable if we are to love, and if others are to love us.

I recently saw a cartoon of a rhinoceros artist. He was happily painting lovely nature scenes in a field, each with a large horn in the middle. It looked strange. I doubt anyone would buy his work. But his art reflected his perception. What he saw was the large horn on his head as a part of every scene he sketched. It was his view of his world. He'd never seen it any other way.

That rhinoceros is less fortunate than you. With the work you're doing right now, you'll be able to remove your child filter and see things differently. But that artist is destined to spend his whole life seeing the world with a horn in the middle.

Chapter 5:
Honor Old Soldiers

Have you heard of the Japanese soldiers on Pacific islands who didn't believe World War II was over? They thought leaflets dropped from planes declaring the end of the war were Allied propaganda. They would not give in. These honorable holdouts prepared each day for any attack that might come, refusing to give up the fight. They couldn't trust the cues around them. They had to hold on. Teruo Nakamura, a Taiwan-born infantryman, held out on the Indonesian island of Morotai until November 1974, nearly thirty years after the end of the war.

Many of us also have those old soldiers still standing guard at the door to our psyche. The poor guys, old and skinny in their dusty uniforms, stand sleepless at the gates, keeping perceived bad things away, protecting us from feelings that threaten. Our soldiers refuse to believe childhood is over, that it is now safe to feel, love, and trust as an adult.

Endearing as they may be, obsolete soldiers bear obsolete weapons. This arsenal can be as benign as the comforting shred of a "blankie" you still carry that helps you feel safe–the same blankie you hid under, singing songs to Teddy as dishes crashed and words exploded outside your door.

But at other times, the soldiers protect with self-destructive behavior.

Take, for example, one young adult victim of childhood sexual abuse. She'd worked through many of the issues and feelings related to her trauma. In most every way, she functioned successfully. She had a good job, friends, and independence. She also carried a hundred extra pounds. Diets, exercise, nothing seemed to help. The excess weight was making her ill and damaging her body.

She continued to find answers in therapy and eventually began to see why she carried that weight. She got to know the old soldier who was her protection. Her unconscious sent the message that if she was obese, it was less likely anyone would want to touch her. Her weight kept her safe. She said the weight felt like "a hug from the inside." The loyal old soldier kept her safe with tins of Rice Krispy treats from the deli and tubs of buttered popcorn at movies she attended alone.

Food, alcohol, phobias, addictions, and psychosomatic illness can all be old soldiers still trying to protect you. As much as you feel ready to lose weight, quit drinking, or get on that plane, you *will not* do it until the soldier is laid to rest and given an honorable hero's farewell.

Someone has to convince him the war is over. You may have to shout in his ear and shake him by the shoulder till dust flies from his uniform. He's probably deaf and blind by now. But do it gently. Set him free in a loving way. Honor that soldier with a moment of silence and a symbolic sendoff. You can take care of yourself now, but thank him for serving.

A relationship with a skilled therapist is helpful in getting these ancient protectors to lay down the sword. Support groups and twelve step programs are also beneficial.

Chapter 6:
Down on the Farm

A nother powerful source of self-sabotage may hold you captive . . . a steady stream of negative self-talk. It runs through your mind like a nagging fourth grade teacher, critical dad, or abusive coach berating you in the silence of your brain. The deafening "noise" drowns out the sounds of happiness that surround you.

It takes time, and emotional investment, to silence old voices that impede your growth. Before you can battle this challenge, you need to gain awareness that it's happening. This is the primary focus. What triggers it? What is its function?

At the beginning you might not even notice its presence. It's just part of who you are. As you gain insight, you begin to hear your mental self-abuse. You see yourself in action. You might even hear yourself use the same words your teacher, coach, or dad used to say.

As an adult, you're free of the toxic relationships that created the mental monologue, but the voices persist. You've not yet learned to function without the negative messages. You don't like to feel criticized, yet it's what you know. It's predictable. There's a degree of contorted comfort in its familiarity.

This inner assault becomes one of the biggest obstacles to freedom. The old messages are still in control, an old habit to break. How can you hear happiness calling with this constant negative chatter? How can you make the choice to leave these old messages behind, and be free?

Once you start to notice the negative self-talk, pay attention to *when* it occurs. It might be a running stream of negativity dosed throughout your day, leaving you feeling apathetic and depressed. Try listening to yourself. When the boss gives you a challenging task, are you telling yourself you'll fail? You receive a compliment. Is there a whisper inside your head saying, "If they only knew. . . . ?"

Or it may rear its head at times when you least expect it. It might happen more often when things are going well, rather than when you're feeling down. You're prepared for a test. You walk into the class feeling confident. You sit down, pencil in hand. Before you look at the first question, that nagging teacher starts chiding you. Your confidence drops as you listen to what a failure you are.

That big interview for the promotion is scheduled. You're qualified and prepared for this new challenge. You've researched the job. You understand the responsibilities. You know you're a good fit. As you enter the interview room, Dad's voice starts muttering "You're a loser." Your posture slumps, and your words become a mumble. All of a sudden, you can't remember any of the statistics you compiled.

On exploration, you may begin to see a connection between times when you're on the verge of success, and the emergence of the negative self-talk. Even as you're feeling positive, confident, and moving forward, the curse sets in. That nagging teacher's voice or parent's words start the retreat to the farm. Once again you've been convinced you aren't smart enough or worthy enough to have good things in your life. Shame builds. Your budding self-esteem seeps out through the old wounds.

When you start to gain insight into the pattern, you can see your unwitting cooperation. With this new awareness, you'll begin to comprehend the function of the negativity. It keeps you stuck in that self-view of failure—down on the farm. There's a part of you that *does* believe you'll never amount to anything. You've been told that all your life, after all. You feel unworthy of good things as long as you're buying into the bad self-talk. If you're stupid, worthless, incompetent, ugly, clumsy, ____ (fill in the blank), how can you be a successful adult?

Do you begin to see your collusion in the conspiracy, and why you believed, in the past, that it was out of your control? As a child you weren't able to stop the negativity others heaped on you. But the fact it holds you back as an adult is something you have the capacity to change.

On exploration, you may find that you hold onto the negative messages because they protect you from the anxiety and fear that accompany bold steps to freedom. You may be like Shel Silverstein's baby bat from *A Light in the Attic* who screams, "Turn on the dark. I'm afraid of the light."[2]

You might argue, "No way. I want more than anything to be successful and strong." Of course . . . but again, only *one part* of you does.

But if you absorb this idea and sit with it, deep down in your secret self it might connect. It's challenging to see the protective nature of this pattern that you want, more than anything, to leave behind. Like that old soldier, this negative self-talk has protected you and kept you safe.

Marianne Williamson, in *A Return to Love,* accurately states, "Our deepest fear is not we are inadequate. Our deepest fear is that we are powerful beyond measure. It is our light, not our darkness that most frightens us."[2]

You can see your power and light only by accepting that it exists. To move beyond old messaging that keeps you from seeing this, you have to face the anxiety that lies beneath—the fear of failure, of freedom, of expectation and accountability. You yearn for freedom, but find it's on the other side of comfort and predictability.

As an undergraduate, I took a criminal justice sociology class. Every day, the professor told us that it's as stressful to be at the front of the pack as it is to be last. As the leader, there's no guide, or bar, or pacer. You're on your own. Along with that frightening reality, there are others behind you, watching and following. What if you make a wrong turn? What if you hit a dead end, or danger, or failure? What if you take everybody off a cliff? This fear can immobilize. You find yourself shrinking from your power, slowing down to be safely tucked in the crowd. In doing so, you diminish yourself, sacrificing power for comfort.

Here's a chance to take your first steps to face your fear. If your decision is to push forward, you encounter the emotional discomfort that accompanies growth and healing.

Psychological putrefaction results from negative self-talk and the burden it creates. Think of it as an "infection" in your emotional wound. It needs to be cleaned out. Envision a runner who falls on a cinder track, her knee torn and bleeding. She washes the wound and applies a bandage, assuming it will heal. It will, but the healing occurs over the imbedded cinders. It looks better at first, but the stiffness worsens, and soon there's smelly yellow gunk oozing out. She breaks down and goes to a doctor. The doc says he needs to clean it out before it can heal right. He says, "Now this is going to hurt a little bit."

And that's what I told my clients. It's going to hurt a little bit emotionally. You have to clean out the old voices and face the fears. In doing so, you let go of the negative stream, and bring healing to an old, putrefied wound of the heart.

Cognitive tools can act as a psychic antibiotic for healing a negative self-talk habit. These tools offer skills to replace a negative message with positive words. We learn to halt the steady stream of negativity that haunts our world by using thought stopping and positive self-talk.

This communication language with self is based on a counseling method called Cognitive Behavioral Therapy, pioneered by Dr. Aaron Beck in the 1960s. Basically, it's learning to change thought patterns in order to change how we feel. It equips us to take inventory of a situation, and step back from negativity supported by early life experiences. We learn to substitute responses appropriate to the situation. With practice, we can shift from the negative interpretation to a more positive reframe.

CBT is designed as a short term, problem-solving therapy. I used it with clients in conjunction with a more relational style, but it was a primary tool for developing positive self-talk. Using cognitive tools, we learn to talk back to the negative message, challenge it, and recognize it as obsolete. From there, we're able to develop a more positive and nurturing script.

As you practice cognitive techniques, you'll be able to take inventory of a situation. For example, you walk into a room where you're meeting two friends. As you enter, you note their bodily tension and frowns. Your instinctive assumption might be that you've done something to upset them. You become defensive and protective before you arrive at the table. But before acting on that gut-level feeling, stop and cognitively examine the scene. What's really going on here? Who's talking? What are they saying or doing? Who is the focus?

From there, you can evaluate your perceptions and feelings. You initially felt threatened, but your inventory of the situation did not identify danger. You recognize this as an old response to similar events. Once you understand that these perceptions are faulty, you can use your self-talk, reframing to reflect more accurately what you're seeing. Then, you can respond to the situation based on its reality. You disconnect it from those feelings from the past. Once you sit down with your friends, you're able to find out what is going on and respond accordingly.

This process involves conversations with yourself. Often, my clients acknowledged they talked to themselves. They would smile and proceed to an old joke, "But, at least, I haven't started to answer myself yet." We chuckled. Then I would say, "Well, now I am going to teach you to answer yourself," and commence their first lesson on the constructive use of self-conversation. They learned the benefits of talking back to the streams of self-incrimination, but only with positive, nurturing words.

As your skill advances in the art of self-talk, you will assess situations and choices you make. But now it will be a real assessment—through adult eyes, without child filters of negativity and fear.

As you continue on your path to authentic self and become a happiness seeker, there's an option to practice along the way. It's a fun, cognitive method of challenging yourself to move forward. It might sound a bit strange, but bear with me.

It's based on the Bob Newhart counseling shtick called "Stop It!" Please take time to watch the YouTube video of this humorous, tongue-in-cheek "therapy mode." My clients were assigned this video. It had its place as a working tool, and provided comic relief in some tense times

In the video, Newhart, the counselor, goes from zero to sixty saying, "Stop It" to a young female client. Remember, it's a comedy routine! No therapist would ever actually do this, but there is a lesson here.

Though done in jest, learning to say, "Stop it" is an effective cognitive technique. It works wonders in short circuiting negative thoughts. When you hear that berating voice in your head, pause and say, "Stop it." It can be yelled, whispered, or telepathically transmitted. It will stall a negative self-talk stream. And a bonus: it will make you smile. "Stop it" is the verbal equivalent of snapping a rubber band on your wrist to break an old habit. It will serve as a reminder if you begin to regress to the negative side.

If a long-term client began that slow slip back to negative self-sabotage, I would just sit and wait. He would soon notice, then smile and say, "I know. Stop it." I would return his smile, and nod. We could move on.

Chapter 7:
Stop the Merry-Go-Round

Have you ever felt you were on a merry-go-round, clinging to a ride called chaos? Toxic behavior and unhealthy relationships can keep us emotionally spinning. How do we slow down enough to put a foot over the edge and slide a sneaker in the dust?

Many of us who grew up in unpredictable situations might be addicted to the chaotic ride. Our childhood brain went into overdrive when there was conflict and turmoil. Our feelings shut down. We numbed up and hung on to keep from falling off. This was an effective skill. When it got crazy, we knew what to do to get through it.

But quiet was ominous. We were left unequipped and vulnerable when all was calm. Our heart wanted to relax and enjoy the peace, but the built-in hyper-alert antenna scanned for early signs of upheaval. Was there a tilt of Mom's head, the crack of a pop-top, was the dog slinking away to his kennel? These were the warning signs we strained not to miss.

Quiet might still create that low level buzz of anxiety. Hypervigilance kept us constantly on the look-out for danger, leaving us in a chronic state of readiness. It served us well as children, but as adults, it gets in the way of a healthy relationship. If we're unaware of its power, we can actually try to recreate chaos and turmoil just to keep that anxiety at bay.

You know those serial rotten relationships, conflicts with coworkers, and family arguments? Once you look at them more closely, you might find *you* are the common denominator.

This doesn't mean you're a trouble-maker or a bad person. It could mean, though, that you feel anxious when the new date is treating you well, or things are going swimmingly at the office or shop. Unintentionally and unconsciously, you may be creating what you are used to, what you know — disarray, pandemonium, turmoil. You unwittingly keep that merry-go-round spinning.

But there's good news. Once you understand the pattern, you begin to see it play out in real time. You can name that restless, edgy tension in your belly. In doing so, you can use cognitive techniques to manage the internal impulses that instinctively rise up. You take responsibility for what you're feeling and consciously make changes to slow the ride down.

You can jump off whenever you want!

Chapter 8:
Scene One–Take Five

We may keep repeating certain behaviors, even though the results are always the same. These cause pain and heartache. They can be present in different forms, but play out most frequently as *unrealistic expectations of others*. This leads to chronic disappointment, self-defeating behaviors, and messages that sabotage our growth.

If we grew up with emotionally unavailable parents, we might have hoped they'd change. But Mom wouldn't give hugs, or Dad never said "I love you." Every day our tender child's heart said, "This time will be different." It never happened. Yet even as an adult, that wistful inner child still hopes Mom or Dad will do the right thing, continuing to set us up for chronic hurt.

This same dilemma keeps us in toxic friendships or romantic relationships. We continue to hope our partner will be respectful and loving, even though he or she has consistently been disrespectful and inattentive to our needs. We wait for the self-centered friend to stop talking endlessly about herself, and to listen to the challenges of our life. Even though it never happens, the child in us keeps waiting.

We walk into hurt and disillusionment every time we expect something people are not capable of giving. We keep hoping for change that never comes.

The real damage of these relationships is how we use them against ourselves. The internal message can reinforce the perception that there's something lacking in us, that *we* are doing something wrong. That if we were just better, prettier, or smarter, or richer, they would treat us differently. Rather than seeing their shortcomings, we continue to feel unworthy and flawed.

The pattern of "scene one—take five" plays out whenever we continue to repeat a behavior we *know* doesn't work, and negatively boomerangs back to us.

It can be minor, like always forgetting to shut a cupboard door, yet each time being surprised when you bang your head on the corner. It seems small, but how about the words you say to yourself (or out loud) every time you hit your head? I'm guessing they aren't very kind.

Or you might take the same route home from work each day, even though the frustrating traffic backs up at the lane merge every time. Rather than acccept this daily slow down, or try another route, you sit in traffic steaming and feeding yourself negative words. This leaves you stressed and angry by the time you get home to children and spouse—every day.

It could be more subtle, like choosing the start of a football game to start sharing your feelings with a football fan partner. A couple once came to me for a counseling session. It was Monday, and they'd fought bitterly the day before. Sherrie tells me she tried to share her feelings with Todd, just as we had practiced. She sat down and faced him, touched his arm and said, "Honey, can we talk?"

And what happened? He rolled his eyes and grunted a pained, "What is it?" She lamented that it was always this way. He shut her down, no matter how hard Sherrie tried to communicate. She sobbed, and Todd looked guilty.

I asked him what had been going on the previous day. He explained that he looked forward to Sunday afternoon football all week. He was settled in with beer and nachos, and his team had made a great kickoff return.

Then Sherrie decides to get deep. He said that if it had been a crisis, he would have responded differently.

But Sherrie said she'd just wanted to practice their communication skills.

After some discussion, we discovered that this was Sherrie's pattern. She typically decided to share feelings when Todd was engaged in something he enjoyed. We examined Sherrie's self-sabotage—how she kept doing the same thing over and over with the same negative consequences. We then explored the further possibility that *she* was the one avoiding communication, but in such a passive way it made *Todd* look like the bad guy. This scene one–take five was blocking their progress to a healthier marriage.

Another "scene one—take five" might be other self-sabotaging behavior that reinforces negative self-messages. Maybe someone's consistently late for a work meeting with the team leader. It always ends badly in the tasks he's given, his evaluations, raises, and lack of promotion. In this case, he unwittingly created the situation, then used it against himself. The message? "I'm a loser. I can't get a break. Something's wrong with me."

Or how about the friend who values reliability and punctuality? Now she isn't returning your calls because you canceled so many lunches at the last minute. It makes you sad. Another friend has abandoned you. It leaves you with the recurrent message that you aren't lovable or worthy of good friends.

The point here isn't to assign blame, but to achieve understanding. As we become more aware of our own role in creating these self-defeating situations, it gives us the opportunity to take ownership of the habit. Once it's ours, we can do something about it. It gives us control. It gives us empowerment.

It gives us *choice.*

Chapter 9:
Respect Where You Are

G ood things happen as you move forward, but you might get frustrated with the pace. Progress is not a straight arrow pointing skyward. It's more like stair steps. You'll have a growth spurt, then level out for a while. It might feel like an eternity before you climb again.

Sometimes the stairs become a Chutes and Ladders game. You make it almost to the top for the win. Then a wrong turn or toss of the dice lands you on a chute, and you slide helplessly back to the beginning. It can be discouraging and disheartening. But remember: Even if you're back at the start, you carry knowledge and insights you learned on that journey to the top. The next climb will be easier.

Sometimes being stuck is functional. There's a reason you aren't getting anywhere. A lesson to be learned. You push and pull. Yet you stay stuck, running around in circles without peace or revelation. It's a challenge to settle in and wait for clarity. It helps to get quiet and accept that you're waiting for something. Trust that you are exactly where you're supposed to be. You'll know when you have gained what you need, and you will feel the freedom of release.

I saw this when I worked with couples. Partners would get frustrated with themselves and each other. In session, goals were set and commitments made for the next week. Maybe it was something as simple as an agreement to take turns with meal preparation or bedtime routine with the kids. These were simple task-oriented goals–nuts and bolts kinds of things. Yet the next time we met, the couple arrived angry and hurt because one or both of them had not followed through with the plan.

As we progressed, it often became clear that a deeper issue was holding them hostage. We took a break from these goals that were leaving them frustrated and discouraged. We stayed where we were to take time to see what would happen. As we explored underlying feelings associated with control and fear, new understandings emerged. They became more vulnerable in their honesty. As they gained insights that were missing before, they were released from old patterns. With that accomplished, the negotiation and compromise of their household roles became a simpler task.

There are many new beginnings and fresh starts that stall out. You'll get exciting ideas that never turn into action. How many New Year's resolutions have you made about food and exercise, or getting more organized, or finishing your degree? "This year I'm going to ____." Whatever fills in that blank was at least an effort at positive change.

You might commit to your health and join a gym, going faithfully for six weeks. You feel positive and strong. Then the fade into the abyss of the snooze alarm begins. The monthly deduction from your bank account marks off a scheduled message of, "I failed again." Or what about the Spanish class you dropped after getting the syllabus, or the watercolor or diving class you bought the equipment for and never attended? And what of the gardening book you purchased and only read one chapter?

They all set in motion a self-improvement exercise. You got a lovely feeling of excitement and anticipation. This is a first step to successful self-care, thinking about being good to yourself and getting excited about trying new things. This is the ladder part of the game we spoke of. You get the anticipatory feeling of accomplishment at the beginning of an idea. But then, after another false start, you feed yourself a stream of meanness, which is the chute that spits you back to the beginning.

In the musical *Oliver*, Fagin dreams of leaving his life of crime and having a normal life. He sings his conundrum in the song "Reviewing the Situation." In each stanza he gets excited about changing his life, making plans and imagining how good it will be. Then the stream of negativity starts, and at the last minute he decides, "I think I'd better think it out again!" He hits that chute. Off he goes back to the life he knows, miserable but predictable. Knowing what to expect is, for him, safer than changing and not knowing what will happen. Like many of us, he fears the change that might set him free, yet he regrets not being able to do it.

Regrets are energy killers. You see that you've fallen short of a goal and ask yourself, "When am I ever going to figure this out?" This begins a stream of toxic self-talk. The first budding efforts at self-love come with a hefty backlash of self-recrimination for past errors, failed efforts, and missed opportunities. This path of negativity subtly supports old feelings of being unlovable and devalued.

Honor your growth curve! When you're ready, it will come. It takes time to get to the deeper emotional connections holding you hostage to these patterns. As your efforts continue, you'll find you are prepared to face the anxiety that accompanies moving into new territory. As you push out of that comfort zone, you will be kinder to yourself, and give grace as needed.

But, for the time being, let's *make use* of these ideas that *don't* get to fruition. Jot them down. In the next section, you can use these as self-care goals and additions to your vision board. That way each false beginning can be reframed into a positive–a future goal that you will one day be ready for.

Learn the art of waiting. It's challenging, but worthwhile. What you learn will surprise you. Trust your rhythm and know success will come. Keep trying. Go for the self-improvements. Remember, even if you don't follow through, *you will learn something in the effort*. When the time is right, you will do the work that moves you beyond this phase. Peace comes with offering your heart the gifts of grace and patience, instead of being that old, harsh self-critic, unforgiving of past failures. Over time, you will become gentler with yourself.

Be cautious of how you view your past mistakes. These can be land mines of self-defeat. Keep the past in perspective. Perhaps when you were in college, you remained in a toxic romantic relationship longer than you can now believe. You knew it was bad, but stayed and stayed. A "last straw" was inevitably broken, and you finally left.

When you examine the feelings about that relationship today, do you beat yourself up emotionally for how long you tolerated being treated badly? Rather than giving yourself a break and being thankful you got free, do you gnash your teeth and berate yourself? Well, instead, how about just sitting with that young college girl who was so sure the guy would change? She made the best choices she knew how to make at the time. Let's give her a break!

This is true for every past error in judgment. I'm talking to you, the guy who ran away from your pregnant girlfriend, or you, the teenage abortion statistic, or the kid who let the buddy take the fall. I understand your feelings of remorse and shame.

But you can find a healthy balance in dealing with past failures and mistakes.

Be sad! Work through the grief and guilt. Make amends where you can. Let the tears of regret trace your cheeks. But *only for so long.* Then it's time to honor who you were, the limitation of your resources, and the truth of your fear.

Forgive yourself. Learn what is to be learned. Lay it down. Let it go. Live your life.

Chapter 10:
Taking the Reins

The first step to managing self-defeating behavior is to develop the insight that *it happens*. Once you recognize its presence, it's easier to manage. You begin to see early warning red flags—a sensation in your stomach, a catch in your throat, an inflection in your voice.

Initially, this awareness might be after the fact. At first that will feel like failure, but use it as a learning opportunity. You have the chance to think about what you could have done differently. Next time you will be more proactive, and another step closer to finding the best tools.

It takes time for new learning to pave a neural pathway in the brain. Think of learning the correct keyboard technique after years of one-finger typing. You were pretty good at getting those reports done using that self-learned skill. Then someone put your ten fingers on that keyboard and said, "Here, let me show you a better way." At first, you were a bumbler and a klutz. But you were shown evidence this could increase your efficiency. You plodded away, error after error. Finally, you learned to keyboard.

The primary path to learning is repetition. That means you have to get the mistakes out of the way! Slowly, with practice, each skill becomes smoother, and you start to improve. But then your supervisor storms in and shouts she needs the report this afternoon instead of tomorrow. Under this pressure, you immediately fall back to the finger pecking, as it's still what you are most comfortable with.

The same thing happens with emotional learning. With practice, you begin to manage negative self-talk and self-defeating behaviors. But let stress and insecurity pile on, and you quickly jump on that critical-coach, nagging-teacher train. It's what you know.

It takes time for a new skill to become set. Honor the learning curve that accompanies any new skill, emotional or otherwise. It takes plodding commitment and perseverance to get to the place you want to be.

You're just beginning to know yourself and why you do the things you do. You're still on a tentative path, insecure in your quest. Sometimes it takes a leap of faith, not knowing where the edge of the cliff lurks. The path won't always be clear. Trust that someone left you crumbs to follow. These may lead you on a path of joyous self-discovery or through a host of struggles. Most journeys are a combination of both.

In the end you'll find your authentic self—a person open to happiness. You'll embrace the small child you once were, your insecure adolescent self, and all your mistakes and successes. You will love you, with all your gifts and challenges, seeing your beauty for the first time.

You'll also become kinder and more accepting of others. You would think that the rosier you see your own loveable self, the more flaws you would find in those around you. But the opposite is true. When you're critical and judging of others, it is through your own filter of feelings of inadequacy. If you expect impossible perfection from yourself, you'll also expect it of those around you. When you give yourself a break, it's paid forward. Once you accept that you are not the best little girl in the world, but not the worst either, you are able to be more relaxed and authentic in relationships.

As you learn the art of self-love, it brings more freedom. It opens your heart to the flirtation of happiness. It takes work to get there, but the benefits are beyond measure. Let go of the illusion that perfection is out there waiting to be found. It's not attainable, and it would be boring if it were.

Being real translates into emotional health, marked by joy, sorrow, fear, courage, and occasional failure. It's more fun than perfection. The good times are sweeter, and the victories more glorious.

The children's book *The Velveteen Rabbit* describes realness:

"'Real isn't how you are made,' said the Skin Horse. 'It's a thing that happens to you. When a child loves you for a long, long time, not just to play with, but REALLY loves you, then you become Real. . . .

'Does it hurt?' asked the Velveteen Rabbit.

'Sometimes,' said the Skin Horse, for he was always truthful. 'When you are Real you don't mind being hurt.'

'It doesn't happen all at once,' said the Skin Horse. 'You become. It takes a long time. That's why it doesn't happen often to people who break easily, or have sharp edges, or who have to be carefully kept. Generally, by the time you are Real, most of your hair has been loved off, and your eyes drop out and you get loose in your joints and very shabby. But these things don't matter at all, because once you are Real you can't be ugly, except to people who don't understand . . . But once you are Real you can't become unreal again. It lasts for always.'"⁴

How does becoming real look for you? Where must you get tattered? How is it going to hurt? How is it going to heal? How is love going to feel?

We all yearn for love that lasts for always and relationships that are true. Yet it's also another one of our greatest fears.

Claiming love is risky. There's vulnerability in trusting someone to love us. We want it. We fear it. Earlier we discussed why we hold on to habits that keep us safe. Some of those protect us from this level of intimacy.

This is where our joints loosen. Being alone or in a toxic relationship is familiar. We know what to expect. Clinging to comfort can keep us in the same spot for a very long time. Moving beyond takes risking emotional safety and stepping out of that comfort zone. Remember it hurts a little to become real, to be open to love.

But it's worth tolerating the anxiety and fear. You'll know when it's time to stand up straight and tall, and walk that road in faith. It's bold. It's scary. It's life-giving. Like so many paths you've traveled, it won't always be clear. You have to follow those crumbs and see where they lead.

Sometimes you find a counterfeit. It may look like a breadcrumb leading your way to love and happiness, but it's just a nut dropped by a squirrel. So what do you do? You say, "Dang it. That's just a nut, and now I've gone off the path." You can be defeated by a squirrel's nut and flee to comfort, or you can laugh at yourself, turn around, and find your crumbs again. The reward at the end of the path is worth it.

Chapter 11:
Things to Consider

B efore leaving this section, I want to address two challenges that might come up as you leave old coping skills behind.

The first is expectation. This new way of living is not a "cure." It is a management tool.

You do not have a disease that requires a cure. You aren't ill. You're just human. You have a life that is a gathering place of all that you have experienced—the good, the bad, the heartbreaking, and the joyful. To erase any of that is to erase a part of you. You would not be who you are right here, right now, without every tiny trace of the life you have lived.

As a result of this truth, the old triggers and defaults that kept your inner child safe may never completely go away. Your brain created this wiring to protect you. The pathways were reinforced as you faced challenges and trauma in childhood.

That wiring might not ever completely disappear. Think of old train tracks, used for years to carry goods across the nation, but that became outdated. Shining, new and faster tracks have been built with stronger metals and computerized signals. The old tracks have remained unused for years. No one's going to try to run a freight on them. Yet they, and their defunct signals, are part of the landscape. Some have been made into biking and walking trails, but the path still remains.

The brain's like that too. In doing the work to break free of the old pathways and tracks, we set up new ones, more functional and better built to handle the weight of adult thinking and coping skills. They're more efficient and stronger. We develop a signal system to navigate the new track.

But those old, outdated routes are still there. Like the life experiences that created them, we can't erase them from our being. What this means is that you may always get a fluttering instinct to flee in response to a perceived threat, or a wave of distrust when you feel vulnerable. You'll sense it as a whisper of negativity, a catch in your chest, a poke at your heart.

It's the call of a ghost memory of the old track[T1]. This is where your new learning, insight, and ability to take control comes in. You ignore the flutter. You recognize the old signal for what it is, an old route — and smoothly transition to the new tracks, following the newly installed adult signals.

It's important to remember this. The goal of this work is not to erase the past. It would change the beauty and intricacy of who you are. Learning the art of self-love enables you to embrace every life experience. With self-understanding, you can enhance your positives and strengths, and manage personal challenges and old messages.

The skills you're learning, and putting into practice, equip you to take control of your life. This allows you to make the choices needed to turn away from the flutters, the catches, and the pokes, and run the train on those beautiful new tracks.

Another factor that can get in your way is your family system. None of us functions entirely as an independent. As you grow and change, you might expect your family to be your greatest support. And consciously they may be. But you may find subtle mixed messages that feel like sabotage to your growth.

This is likely not just your imagination. You're all parts of a system that functions well when all the cogs are doing their job. When you change, you quit fitting as well in this unconscious mechanism of family. The whole system feels it. Unwittingly, they try to pull you back into that functioning. It's not that they discourage your growth, but if you change then the whole rest of the system has to transform too. If change is thrust on any of us against our will, it's seldom well received deep down in the belly.

A family of an alcoholic is an excellent example. There's tremendous distress, worry, and pain in these families. The greatest desire is that the identified patient, the alcoholic, gets help and quits drinking. But when that finally occurs, no matter how much better life is for everyone, there are subtle actions in the family that feel like sabotage to recovery. The entire system was built around coping with an alcoholic. Now that function is no longer needed.

You will sometimes hear alcoholism discussed as a family illness. That's why Twelve-Step programs try to include all family members, not just the drinker. Everyone knows about Alcoholics Anonymous, and Narcotics Anonymous, for substance abusers. But there is also Al-Anon and Alateen, programs to help family members learn how to stop enabling and being part of the system, but also assist in letting go of that system when recovery and sobriety begin. Good alcohol and drug treatment programs include regular family sessions and groups to help a recovering alcoholic or addict re-enter the family.

Another example is the obese family. Mom and Dad, and siblings have a history of weight issues and the health challenges that result. The family functions around food. What happens when you decide to take control of your health and work hard to get to a healthy weight? Everyone cheers you on, and is happy for you as you go down in sizes and get more active. They see the difference. They express their support. You're excited and start to encourage the whole family to eat healthier, and exercise with you.

But you begin to notice that your favorite restaurants are frequently selected for dinners out. The maple glazed donuts you used to crave start showing up at breakfast. Mom makes your favorite five-cheese and cream-based macaroni and cheese once a week now. All coincidence? Likely not. Your success is acting as a mirror to the family. You're making everyone uncomfortably aware of his or her own issues. The family system is being disrupted, and *you* are the cog that is causing the dislocation.

These situations create challenges as we work to make changes. We're called to even greater insight, commitment, and perseverance.

It's important to remember you can change only yourself. You can't impose change on others. Even if you aren't, consciously, trying to do that, those around you are impacted just the same, and some will fight the magnetic pull of change.

The disruption of function upsets the whole system—unless the family can repair itself by pulling you back to the way things were.

It's helpful to be aware of your own sense of abandonment and rejection as you move away from a family system. It's been your place of comfort and shelter, after all.

In that case, look elsewhere for the support you need to continue your growth. The best thing you can do for your family meanwhile is to talk to them, and set clear boundaries. Let them know how much you love them, but also help them understand how important these changes are for you.

If you can stay on course and withstand the magnetic familial pull, you'll succeed. As an added bonus, if you're faithful to your growth, others may slowly begin to make changes also. But it has to come from them. You can't make it happen until they are ready.

One partner would come in to my office for individual counseling, even though there was a relationship issue. At first, her primary goal was to transition to couples work. She believed nothing could be done if the other partner refused to take part.

But individuals can make a difference in a partnership if one client's truly willing to look hard at his or her role in the marital dysfunction. A great deal of work can be done, as one partner learns how to manage his or her own behavior. This might involve learning how to avoid creating chaos, managing defensiveness, or simply becoming kinder. By being consistent in these changes, new boundaries are being unconsciously established. The other partner slowly begins to change in response.

A pastor friend once shared a story. A woman came to ask for his blessing for her decision to divorce her husband. She couldn't tolerate the loveless, verbally abusive situation any longer. The pastor responded that he wanted her to try something for three months. He asked her to behave in the most loving manner she could toward her husband, to treat him as she had when they first met. Then she was to come back to meet with the pastor. If at that time, there was no change in her marriage, he would bless her decision to divorce.

What the pastor was really asking her to do was to step out of the family system she and her husband had unconsciously created.

Three months passed as she did what he asked. Then the wife returned to the pastor's office. He asked her how it had gone. She told him she couldn't believe she'd ever thought about divorce. Over the past three months, he'd gone back to being the man she'd married. He was loving, full of laughter, and kind. She told the pastor it was a miracle. God had changed her husband.

God might have had a hand in it, but I suspect it was primarily the woman's actions that brought out the goodness and love from her husband's heart once more. She pulled herself out of the system of dysfunction. Her change in behavior and attitude toward him and their marriage paved the way for his changes. Yes, this story may have a degree of exaggeration to make a point, but I think it's a point well taken.

Chapter 12:
Soaring to Happiness

I hope the information and assignments in the previous chapters were helpful. The goal was to increase insight into why some things are hard, and create awareness of roadblocks that keep us stuck. We looked at the value of embracing our inner child, and feeling our childhood pain and loss. That required emotional risk and vulnerability—the first steps to healing.

Now, on to the next stage in learning how to be your best self. The journey requires perseverance. It's important to respect your growth curve and move at your own pace. Keep your timeline handy, and use it as needed. The keys are commitment and practice. There's knowledge to gain and skills to learn. Take a deep, cleansing breath. Close your eyes, and visualize smooth sailing ahead.

I want to present two concepts in this part of the book. Both help create a lifestyle that invites happiness. These skills provide a healthy base for continued growth. They are the art of self-care and the practice of mindfulness. You're probably familiar with both, but I want to emphasize and elevate their importance. I consider these concepts the mama and papa of emotional health—the basic tools for deeper healing.

First, we'll look at the art of self-care. How you treat yourself impacts how you feel about yourself. The messages you send to yourself about your worth and value affect self-esteem more than any other single factor. The words and actions of others can provide validation and support, but you must be your own best friend and cheerleader.

Chapter 13:
The Oxygen Mask

The instructions for use of an oxygen mask on a commercial airliner are a good illustration of the value of self-care. Flight attendants mime the tutorial as the plane taxies down the runway. The part to focus on is, "Always put your oxygen mask on first before assisting others."

Simply put, you can't help someone else if you've passed out. I would like, just once, to see the miming go to the extent that the attendant puts the mask on someone else, grabs her own throat, bugs her eyes out, and falls to the floor. This would be a true illustration of how things would go if she made that fatal error.

It's the same if you don't take care of yourself, only more insidious. Emotional self-care is as life sustaining as oxygen, just less obvious. There are immediate consequences to oxygen deprivation. You have to breathe. You know right away if there's a problem. I wish self-care also had some signal of imminent demise if you went without it for too long.

Taking care of yourself is an alien concept if you've never taken time for you. The self-nurturing litany might make you uncomfortable. The thought of putting yourself first seems selfish and greedy. You heard early messages telling you all love was conditional—maybe not in words, but in looks, and shrugs, and shaking heads.

You figured out what you had to do to earn it. To be loved, you had to focus on pleasing others. The best behaved, the easy child, the kid that stayed out of trouble? Was that you? The effort was exhausting. No matter how hard you tried, you never felt good enough because you could never seem to do enough. You could never be perfect. The focus remained on what everybody else needed, and what everyone else expected you to be. You didn't learn much about meeting your own needs.

If this old message carried over to adulthood, you continued the cycle. You ignored your own needs in the sacrificial acts of the pleaser.

Years of this behavior can leave you spiritually and emotionally starved. The first step to discovery comes in the form of dawning awareness. In the short term, you may note how tired you really are, and how little you know about what makes you feel good—besides validation from others. Don't be discouraged. Awareness has to emerge before you can step onto a different path. As you begin to pay attention to the many facets of your own humanness, that insight will increase. Then you'll begin to create your own definition of self-care. The concept is personal and has many layers. Embrace it as your own.

The basic meaning of self-care is simple. All of us take some degree of care of ourselves. As children, we acquire the fundamental activities of daily living. We learn to feed, clothe, and clean ourselves. Growing up, we refine these, and move on to advanced skills like managing jobs and homes.

But what about the skill of honoring and attending to our own emotional needs? This goes beyond the basics. This is higher-level learning, and a vital component of a healthy lifestyle. The art of self-nurturance provides balance and harmony.

It feels good to think about taking better care of yourself, to envision what it would look like. Like everything else, no matter how much you want to do this, it takes time. It requires self-knowledge and skill to push beyond those roadblocks on your path. As always, be patient with you, and trust that it will come.

Remember, only you are equipped to figure out what you need. This book can offer guidance, but no one knows you better than yourself. This is a personal, unique study. No two of us have the same set of needs. There is no single formula, only a template. As you create your plan, you'll get excited as you begin to discern what works.

One goal of the previous section was to provide the opportunity to understand and embrace that authentic you — the good, the bad, and the average. With that increased awareness, you can design the self-care shelf of your future toolbox.

Two important components of emotional self-care are validating feelings and setting healthy boundaries. With time, you'll be able to acknowledge your feelings, and speak up for yourself, saying no when necessary.

Validation of feelings and healthy boundaries work together. In order to set effective boundaries, you must first believe your feelings, needs, and personal space are of value. If you were raised on the "Don't talk. Don't trust. Don't feel" mantra, you did not have a safe environment to develop these skills. You were afraid to acknowledge or express what you held inside, labeling it as bad or wrong. You coped by stuffing those untouched feelings and doing what others expected.

Each time you were silent, it reinforced the self-message you were not good enough — not worthy of being heard. On the rare occasion someone affirmed your words or apologized for hurting you, you didn't quite believe it.

As an adult, it can still feel unsafe if you live by the rules of these old messages. There's emotional risk in stepping out of that comfort zone. The first step is learning to honor your feelings, your values, and your "you". From there, you'll begin to acknowledge feelings without passing judgment on yourself. You'll find the freedom to give feelings a voice. By doing this, you become your biggest fan. You carry your own torch.

Setting personal boundaries validates your right to say no. That "no" is the tip of the boundary iceberg, the prerequisite to further study of the art. You will develop the ability to stand up and mark your personal space with words and actions. This helps you create your edges, the ability to be separate from others in a healthy way. Once you get to that place, others around you sense it. An energy emanates from you that elicits respect. Call it an aura, body language, or a glitter in your eye. It's there, and others pay attention.

I call it clear versus cloudy edges. The person with clear edges sets healthy personal boundaries. In my life experience, I always knew where I stood and what to expect from that clear-edged person, as well as what was expected of me. It gave me a sense of my own position in relation to theirs. It felt safe. When around cloudy-edged people, I never knew what to expect, and there seemed to be a hum of chronic tension. I decided early on that I wanted those clear edges, and to be around those I felt most safe and comfortable with. I also want that for you.

Setting boundaries was a new concept for me when I first started this work. As a kid, already the family therapist, I was the caretaker of others and the gatekeeper of calm. Taking care of people, and the occasional stray cat or dog, was what I knew. It was tied up in my self-worth. It took work, with my own therapist, to quit trying to save my family. I had to grab that oxygen mask and breathe in the life giving air. In the process, I learned to use my challenge as a gift that enhanced my professional work.

The level of ease with which a new client adjusted to self-nurturing indicated how our work would progress. Claiming an hour of counseling to talk about yourself seems extravagant, selfish, and terribly uncomfortable. Yet, like the work you're doing here, it is often the first effort at putting on the oxygen mask.

Yes, the therapy hour is hard to claim. There might be late cancellations of appointments because mother, brother, or random person on the street needed a ride, or late arrivals because a phone call couldn't wait. These became therapy issues, objective learning opportunities to work through the sludge of misguided servanthood that can block happiness.

We must learn to make a choice. Is the other person's need more important than our own? We may still choose to cancel or be late, or sacrifice any number of things. But the critical factor is choice. Most of us don't think in terms of choice. We immediately say yes, dropping our plans in order to meet someone else's needs. It's important to learn how to step back and take time to choose. It's empowering and validating.

It is helpful to find proactive ways to manage this challenge. A wise colleague once told me the best statement we can ever learn is, "Let me get back to you on that." These magic words provide breathing space to think about how we feel and whether we want to say yes or no. It takes us one step back from the default "OK, sure." It gives us back control. It gives power. It gives choice.

***

Exercise 4: In a counseling relationship, we explored underlying feelings and fears that held clients hostage to this exhausting cycle. Take out your timeline, and do some of your own exploration. You'll find clues there. Look at the events placed above the line and the feelings below. Are there times you remember words not spoken and feelings not expressed? Do you remember how you felt emotionally or physically at those times? If feelings or new memories come up, go ahead and note these on your timeline.

***

Pay attention, in the here and now, to how often you say "yes" when you want to say "no." Get in touch with how you feel when this happens. Does it stick in your throat a little? Do you get a headache or gut ache?

Discover what the desire to say "no" feels like. You'll start to recognize early warning signs that you're saying "Sure, whatever" when you want to say "No way!" Does "OK" come out with symptoms of resentment? Do you feel powerless? Sad, anxious, or ill? A migraine or stomach ache is a physical manifestation of a "yes" person's silent scream.

Take stock. What percentage of your time is taken up by events and activities you agreed to against your will? Are you at the top of the list at work, church, and family gatherings? You know, that list of folks who always say yes. I spent a while on that list myself. I spent years room-mothering and organizing family events. I had my own list, too. I knew who would help. I always called them first. They always agreed. They may have looked haggard on arrival, but the covered dish or centerpiece was always delicious or perfect.

How much free time do you have to spread around? How much of that do you take for yourself? Part of the answer may be based on your season of life. If you're a single working person or retiree, your time available is far different from the single parent with three kids under five. Don't be discouraged if you're in the latter category. Ultimately, the amount of time you have is less important than how you use it. I taught many busy moms and dads how to do five-minute meditations, time-outs in the bathroom, and dances with the vacuum. It's about how you use what time you have. Is it nurturing, honoring, and restorative? Then it's right. The more the better, but a little bit will do—if you do it right.

Self-assessment of need is critical. It helps you gain insight into how serious this issue is for you. If you don't manage the overload with sufficient self-care, you could become ill. The body seeks wellness and balance. For a long time, that means it adapts to chronic exhaustion. But at some point, the brakes lock and skid you into the ditch.

Think of a frog in water. The story goes, if you place a frog in a pan of hot water, he'll jump out. He senses its danger and knows to get away. But if you sit the little guy in a pan of cold water on low heat, he'll settle in. The water slowly heats up, but his body adapts. There are no warning signs until it's too late.

Fortunately, our bodies respond quicker than a frog's. Our physical self usually gets us out of hot situations before we're cooked. But the body can be pushed past its limits just so long. Then it takes control. Once the immune system is compromised from chronic stress and fatigue, our miraculous physical self begins to say no. We may try to say yes with words, but any number of symptoms start to set up roadblocks until we end up in bed or the hospital.

If you are running on empty, you have nothing left. You are past "E." Even then, you might not be aware of exhaustion and the resentment building a negative fire in your belly. You continue to push yourself to please others.

To complicate things, our current society tends to portray busyness as a badge of honor. We compete for who works the hardest, does the most, and has their kids in the most activities. There seems to be a stigma if we're found sitting quietly reading a book or napping.

Before change can occur, we need to take this trait out of the status realm of noble and sacrificial. We may unconsciously see our lack of boundaries as a special, sensitive trait that ranks us a notch above others. We're the selfless ones. Yes, there's something about being chronically depleted that feels heroic, or even saintly. But . . . remember the "Stop it" routine? I am telling you, in a most loving way, to just "Stop it."

There's nothing emotionally, spiritually, or mentally healthy about chronic exhaustion. It takes time to understand that this is actually self-sabotaging behavior. It's critical to see it for what it is . . . an issue that impedes growth and blocks happiness. It's damaging to physical health. It leaves us empty.

Just writing that paragraph wore me out, because I remember how true it was for me!

You may silently wish others would give you a break and not expect so much. But you can't change the persons benefitting from your lack of boundaries. As I told my clients, why would those around you want anything to change? We humans are like an electric current, traveling the path of least resistance. If someone will pick up after me and do whatever is my bidding, who am I to ask them to stop? I may offer an occasional, "Oh you shouldn't have," but I'll go right on accepting the service.

I saw this pattern often in couples with young children. During the first sessions, they might identify the issue as a poor sex life. Over time it became clear that the stay-at-home mom was shouldering all the household responsibilities and child care. Dad worked all day outside the home, and came home at night to relax. She resented that he never helped with the house or kids. Yet, she never expressed her feelings or needs. As her unspoken resentment increased, it became a relationship issue that played out in the bedroom.

With time, we worked on boundaries and communication. Once she was able to name her needs, things improved quickly. Dad took over the toddler and baby when he got home. Mom got a break. Baby bedtimes went more smoothly, leaving the two of them some couple time before bed. The intimacy returned. Looking back, they could see their warped roles. She didn't let him know what she needed from him. Although he saw her fatigue, it didn't occur to him to jump in and help when he came home from work tired himself.

Once you learn to state your needs, "yea" will mean "yea," and "nay" will mean "nay." You will start to set solid boundaries and stick to them. Others will slowly adapt to the fact that you mean what you say. You will gain respect from others and yourself as you become the one with the clear edges.

In the early phase of practicing this skill, be cautious where you draw the lines in the sand. Don't draw one you know you're going to cross. I tended to let these lines get crossed when my children were small. After starting yet another chore chart for my boys, my youngest son groaned about the new responsibilities. His wise, older brother said, with a knowing smile, "Don't worry. It won't last very long." Busted. They were on to my pattern of enforcement cycles, and my lines in the sand, which lasted only about three weeks.

Beware. Like the boy who cried wolf, your words quickly, lose credibility. Your confidence dwindles proportionately. You will be seen as a pushover, once again. Worse—you'll feel like one. Start with easy boundaries, such as "No, I do not have time to pick up the milk." You will still want to pick up the milk. You will want to, badly. But, do not stop to get milk. Do not stop at the neighbors to borrow milk. Do not repeatedly apologize for not stopping to pick up milk.

Slowly, you will gain confidence in your skill. You'll be able to make bolder statements. Then, if needed, it will be time to move on to the boundaries that carry more emotional risk such as, "I cannot be with you any longer if you continue to behave in this manner."

As you learn the skill of boundary-setting, changes will occur. You will note stronger self-esteem, increased energy, and you'll feel better physically. Over time, you'll feel less depressed and anxious. All that energy expended on pleasing others, hiding resentment, and burying feelings is now available to use as you choose.

When you feel good about who you are, you are more open with others, creating closer relationships. I don't know about you, but none of that sounds selfish to me. The ironic benefit of this work is that you become a truly giving person. As you learn to express your feelings and tell people what you need and do not need, you'll experience a growing desire to do kind and loving acts. These kind acts will be freely given in love, not yielded reluctantly in emotional slavery. You will choose to be there for others.

You might offer to take a friend to a medical appointment, make a meal for a sick neighbor's family, or use a precious vacation day to docent at the zoo. The essence of these acts is different. You choose to sacrifice your energy and free time. You authentically care. Freely given acts of kindness nurture the heart. They don't deplete you like the constant need to please. You might feel physically tired, but you wear the smile of someone touched by happy. It's all about the spirit of the gift. It's all about choice.

Empowered, you can open your heart to bountiful doses of happiness that you pass on to others. You will find yourself living that life of compassion and substance, the life well-lived that Emerson spoke of.

Look at your patterns. Be honest. Are you a yes person? If you're nodding and groaning, recognizing yourself, take heart. I'll provide some helpful tools later. For now, here is an assignment. Let's get serious about staying fueled and fully functional!

***

Exercise 5: With this assignment, you'll begin to draft a basic self-care plan. It is the beginning of your special time and special space. We will also do more work on these later in the tools section.

As you work on this assignment, focus on yourself—what you want to do and how you would like to feel. This will become a guide to your personally tailored self-care goals.

First, think about what feels relaxing. Go back in the recesses of your memory. Recall a time you read in the park or soaked in a bubble bath a few years ago. Think about what activities you enjoyed as a child. What was on the list of "What I want to do when I grow up"? Think about what you want to do after the kids are grown or when you retire.

Start making a list. It might take a while to recall what excited and energized you. Doodle, draw flowers, and hum as you think. Your memory search will start to give way to old dreams and aspirations.

Write down everything that comes to mind, even the ones that aren't currently attainable. Don't censor yourself. For example, I dreamed of being a famous ballerina. That I never had a childhood ballet lesson, was decidedly uncoordinated, and am too old to start now, decrease my chances to dance in the New York Ballet. But that's never stopped me from enjoying a ballet. When I was thirty, a friend and I took private lessons from a locally renowned dance teacher. Some days I felt like a butterfly. Other days I was a bulldog. Some days we were serious students. Other days we took our teacher to a nearby restaurant, and ate cinnamon rolls, bacon, and cocoa. No judging! It was my fantasy. I got to do what I wanted. So, I will never be a ballerina, but I can still plié. And I continue to attend the ballet. I remain awed by its beauty and grace. Though I did not literally fulfill my dream, I did find a way to use it that pleases me, gives me joy, and brings me peace.

Your dreams, fantasies and aspirations don't have to be directly attainable, but naming and claiming each one will allow you to explore how they can fit into your life. This could take several brainstorming sessions, but eventually you'll realize you're finished—for the time being.

Next, take the brainstormed list and refine it. What can you do right now without any adjustments to your situation? These may include activities as simple as sitting on the back porch for five minutes, or using a special scented body wash in your quick shower. Maybe there's music you'd like to listen to on the drive to work, the kind made for loud sing-a-longs and steering wheel drums. Maybe you'd like to eat lunch on a bench in the park—you know, the spot where crimson and gold maple leaves once fell at your feet? Or, what about that spring walk in the woods a few years ago—the one where all the trees seemed to green up all at once?

Start simple. Circle these easy-to-do moments. Put stars and diamonds and smiley faces around them with colored pencils. Make this a fun exercise, a tiny step in bringing joy to yourself and letting that child within you play. If you let your child in on the planning, she will release you to think outside the box. The adult "you" may have a nagging feeling that you're "wasting time." Ignore that voice telling you to go do something constructive. This exercise is the most important thing you can do right now. It's a budding step in self-care and claiming personal self-worth.

Start with this short list of the here-and-now items. A list of less than ten is a good place to start. You could feel overwhelmed by good choices, if you have more. You can add to them as you get more proficient at being good to yourself.

Do NOT throw away the brainstormed list. You'll return to it often. Put it in your special stuff drawer. Prioritize the doable list by numbering the items. Make sure the list includes healthy activity, quiet time, and fun stuff. Put your name at the top of the page in gold glitter.

The brainstorming list will be another living document you will continue to use. Get it out, occasionally, as you proceed on your journey. Play with your list. Refine it. Add to it. Sit back and smile at it.

Chapter 14:
The Value of Right Now

The second gift vital to your happiness pursuit is mindfulness. It offers a pathway to full presence in your life. It's a form of self-care, but also a means of relating to others and the world.

Before we proceed, a cautionary note. This is going to sound easy. It's not. There is much distraction in our world that diverts us from noticing the simple joys that are available to us. There are constant stimuli from multiple sources. Sometimes our brains are so full that we're on automatic pilot. Have you ever washed an entire sink of dishes and realized that you never once paid attention to what you were doing?

Learning to see what's around you is like refocusing the brain to see hidden pictures or optical illusions. You have to stop and focus from a different perspective before the image is revealed. Your frontal lobe starts to feel fuzzy and pressured. Then, all at once, the world shifts. You see what you were missing.

That's the way it is with mindfulness. Like so many things already discussed, it requires retraining, but it's worth the effort.

Many have described mindfulness and its practice, but I hesitate to make it small by boxing it in with words. This is not about how to be mindful in six easy steps. It's about the emotional essence of the term, rather than any logical understanding. How it manifests, and how it feels when you get there.

But we start with the basics, so here's a brief definition. Keep in mind that it is more than any words can illustrate and more difficult than it sounds. The professional journal *Psychology Today* answers the question, "What is mindfulness?" with: "Mindfulness is a state of active, open attention on the present. When you're mindful, you observe your thoughts and feelings from a distance, without judging them good or bad. Instead of letting your life pass you by, mindfulness means living in the moment and awakening to experience."[3] This self-care practice is a key to peace. With it you can embrace all the little living noises around you, many of which are sources of happy moments.

Mindfulness as a stress management tool has become a primary focus in the medical and mental health communities. This is a step forward, because practitioners are learning to identify stress as a causal factor of illness. There's also much written on the topic in magazines and wellness programs. It's a positive step that there's more information becoming available on this critical issue.

At the same time, a caution. I'm protective of mindfulness. We Americans tend to get excited about a concept as it becomes more popular. Then, filled with good intentions, we market it to death with business ideas, advertising, and promotion. I'm trying to avoid that pitfall. As we proceed, I promise not to recommend any special pants to wear or props to purchase. You need nothing but yourself and your intention. You don't even need to set aside a special time for many forms of mindfulness. It's available every minute of every day. All you have to do is learn to focus in order to see what it offers.

Mindfulness is being in the moment. It's the ability to let go of past mistakes and worry of the future. It lets go of the to-do list running through your brain that shotguns your calm. Mindfulness offers softness and vulnerability. It creates awareness of the miracles around you, opening your heart to joy. It is meditative and relaxing. And it leads to less stress, improved health, and deeper relationships. This practice opens a window to a profound appreciation of life in real time.

A mindfulness practice opens us up to beauty and joy, but it is also a tool to be used in managing pain and discomfort. Pain of any nature can leave us feeling helpless, creating stress and tension. If we have physical or psychic discomfort, sitting with the pain, exploring it, and being fully present in it allows us a means of control. Practicing mindfulness with pain, whether a headache, hurt feelings, poison ivy, anxiety, or a chronic illness, allows us the power of exploration. Is it a throb? A heat? A pin prick? In approaching pain with curiosity and attentiveness, we can leave behind agitation and helplessness, both contributors to the intensity of pain.

Mindfulness also benefits our eating habits. A mindful focus as we eat helps us take time with food. Mindless eating often leads to overeating, and ingesting unhealthy junk. Generally we eat too fast, which is bad for digestion. When meals or snacks are bolted while we're doing something else, the brain doesn't register the intake. Fullness signals don't kick in, so we keep on noshing.

How often do you find yourself standing at the kitchen counter, eating something you've grabbed out of the pantry or refrigerator? Or spending the evening watching television with a bag of chips by your side? When you finish your movie, you find the bag empty. If asked in either of these situations, you probably wouldn't be able to describe what you ate or how it tasted. If you're an emotional eater who tends to overeat when angry or sad, this habit is especially troublesome.

Mindfulness provides structure and time. If you want to eat intentionally, set the table with plate, silverware, and napkin. Fresh flowers and candles make a lovely add-on. Eat slowly, taking time to chew each bite. Sense the food in your mouth. Pay attention. Is it sweet or salty? How does the texture feel on your tongue? Appreciate the food, the cook, and the plants or animals that were used in the preparation. By doing so, you respect the ritual of mealtime, and everything and everybody that contributed. When food is experienced in this way, it's a nurturing experience—physically, sensually, and spiritually.

We can be mindfully present in many ways. I will break down the practice into three levels, from the informal to the more structured. The points are on a continuum and blend into each other. They can be tailored to your needs, as you take into account your own lifestyle, life stage, and current situation.

The least formal is Passing Mindfulness. This form can become a constant in your daily life. When passively mindful, you're fully present during work, play, or quiet. You can be mindful while cleaning the bathroom or taking out the garbage. It's a state of being you carry with you throughout the day.

Passing Mindfulness can be enhanced and nurtured in many ways. Some find outdoor exercise helpful. Others like to sit quietly in a special space. When my children were young, I wrote about peaceful time in my one quiet place—the laundry room. Later, I wrote about feeling closest to God when I ran. These times stirred creativity and peace. I instantly recognized them as special. Now I see these were Passing Mindful moments.

The beauty of mindfulness is that it's a multi-sensory experience. It gives you the ability to hear the range of mockingbird chirrups or notice leaves whispering to the wind.

It offers the colors changing as the sun moves across the ornamental grasses, or the feeling of the fluff of your kitten's soft fur. It's watching a baby sleep with his or her fluttering eyelashes and half-smiling lips. It's wrapped in wind chimes and an exquisite taste on your tongue. Passing Mindfulness gives you the ability to see the happiness that's out there waiting. All you have to do is notice.

In *One Thousand Gifts*, Ann Voskamp[6] recommends making a list of the many gifts you see, hear, and feel. She cites moments as huge as her son's growth to manhood and as miniscule as holding an opalescent soap bubble in her hand as the sun's rays reflect within it. We forget that there's meaning in the minutiae. It's often these fleeting memories that flash in our brain when we reflect on our lives.

We have momentous occasions imbedded in our heart, but the effortless just-let-things-pop-into-our-head times bring a flood of tiny bursts that bloom like heart blossoms. Sit quietly and close your eyes. Reflect silently on the images immediately rising to the forefront of your brain. What mindful gifts do you remember?

In my moment, I see picture frames of children's laughter and lazy mornings of unstructured play. Kids and dogs run through the house like herds of happiness. I watch feasts for stuffed animal menageries, rocket rides from living room chairs, and camp-outs under tablecloth tents. These are moments I noticed—first crocuses peeking through late-winter snow, spring rain on daffodils, downhill bicycle rides, fishing ponds, hot-coffee mornings around a campfire, and the internal butterfly kiss of a baby's first kick. My heart found peace in the stillness of a snow-covered stand of north-country woods and the marsh-scented humidity of a low country dawn. My spirit was cleansed by seaside sunrises, and prepared for rest by the crunch of crisp autumn leaves under my boots. I would have missed each precious one of these passing moments, had I been too busy.

I grieve the ones I did miss. You know those times—a bad day, too many tasks, preoccupation with our worries about tomorrow or regrets from yesterday. These take us away from the present. We miss magic. We miss meaning. We lose blissful moments that crystallize into fireflies of happiness.

Sometimes we become more open to these moments of passing mindfulness when we're reminded life is precious. We all have a story about a near miss that wakes us up to this lovely world. Following a close call, everything looks sweeter. We see life differently for a while. Each day becomes meaningful in a shiny, shimmering way. We view life through gratitude goggles, seeing only what is important. These times may last only a little while. After a fender bender that could have been much worse, you hug your partner, kids, and dog tighter. You're so grateful just to be alive and in one piece.

After a few days of whining children and complaining coworkers, though, the glow starts to wane. Daily demands and grumpy negativity set in, and you leave the gratitude goggles on the back of the bathroom toilet. They lie forgotten among the tissues and air freshener, until another scare comes along.

Then comes a lump under the skin that leads to an uncharted path of sickness and fear. There's no quick resolution or instant relief. This time, you don't know if you'll survive. It's a journey no one chooses to take, but you have no choice. It takes you along on a ride of quiet terror and steadfast resolve. Months later, you wake up on the other side and see that the sun shines brighter. You really do live each moment as if it may be your last. This time it does not fade. Each morning you give thanks for the miracle of your heart beating and the breath you breathe. It is a metanoia experience. You are changed. You see every moment and grasp every flirtation that happiness hands you.

But we don't have to have a life changing experience to live like this. Buddhist teachings instruct us to live our lives with an awareness of life's impermanence. This means understanding that this moment, kiss, pain, wealth, or chocolate won't last. It also makes us aware that, at any given second, this earthly life, itself, may cease to exist. At first blush this seems pessimistic, but if practiced, it brings a sweetness to all experience as we value each minute.

Attitudes change when we view each day as precious. We're more positive, thoughtful, kind. Some days it will come naturally. Other times it takes a conscious decision to see the good in the day, but it is always attainable. It is always worthwhile.

***

Exercise 6: This simple exercise sets the intention of the day to Passing Mindfulness. It reminds us that we get to choose our focus every morning.

Our tendency is to set the alarm for the very last minute and hit the floor already frazzled. I ask you to give up fifteen minutes of sleep. It will become the most valuable time of your day.

Each morning before getting out of bed, close your eyes and envision your day. In these moments you set the course of this special day, the one and only "this day" you will ever have. Spend the moment just being. Take a deep breath. Stretch. Smile to yourself as if you carry a special secret. Think of something lovely.

Then, sit up and slowly put your feet on the floor. Sit on the edge of your bed for a few seconds. Stretch your arms over your head and take another deep breath. Whisper to yourself "What a lovely day it's going to be, and I'm not going to miss any of it."

You have just set your course to a mindfully present day.

In these few minutes, you set yourself in a more positive direction, bringing a level of lightness to your spirit. You let go of burdens you didn't know you had. Peace comes in that letting go. This is where mindfulness has its power.

Remember to continue the practice of Passing Mindfulness as you go about your day.

***

The second level is Purposeful Mindfulness. You stop to smell the roses a little longer and with more intention. You become a bit more organized and structured in staking a claim to peace. For illustrative purposes, I'll continue with the early morning prescriptive.

***

Exercise 7: This assignment requires a little more time. You'll need to set your alarm thirty minutes earlier for this exercise. Do the same stretching and getting out of bed. But from there find a space in the house or porch, and take a few minutes to sit. Close your eyes and take six deep even breaths. Do a slow cadenced count of "in-two-three-four, out-two-three-four" with each inhale and exhale. This paces your breathing and draws your focus inward.

After you've done six of these breaths, just sit with your eyes closed for a couple minutes. Set the intention of your day as you did in the previous exercise.

***

This practice gives you more space to experience calm. It also adds the gift of breath. You're more intentional in setting your focus. This early morning exercise sets your day at a low baseline stress level. As a result, you'll find yourself less reactive to stressful situations as your daily routine progresses. You can't avoid stress, but you can manage it.

This is an excellent tool to use throughout the day, wherever you go. You can always find time for two minutes to close your eyes and breathe to "reset" yourself. It re-centers and calms. As you adapt Purposeful Mindfulness, I encourage you to include time outdoors and intentional quiet time in your plan. This can take any form that works for you. If you're a runner, you know what a run on a trail will do. But if you're a busy mom or dad, with little time, you can take two minutes to step out on the back porch, breathe in the fresh air, and let the breeze wisp your hair.

Remember, quality versus quantity. Don't be tempted to sacrifice yourself to the detriment of your health. It's too easy to let other things take precedence over your needs. Choose to claim time.

You can probably tell I'm a morning person, since most of these exercises commence at daybreak. My whimsical side envisions angels who come out at night, as we sleep, to clean up the human clutter that litters our days. The early morning is fresh and pure, untouched and new. I've spent quiet time with the sunrise for so long I don't remember what life was like without it.

But you may be a second shift worker, parent up all night with babies, or just a person who doesn't like to see the day until ten a.m. Use your imagination. Adapt these assignments and illustrations to your situation and schedule. The simple act of doing that will make you feel more in control of your life.

I call the third level a Formal Practice of Mindfulness. This level entails the most time and intent. It's the process of developing a daily meditation practice. You will set aside one to two times a day for a twenty-minute meditation. Later, we'll look at some different techniques and how to create your space. Rather than a specific exercise for a formal practice, I'll try to give you a sense of what to expect at this level.

For now, the goal is to consider a meditation practice that brings quiet and calm. At the end of a full meditation, you are more alert and aware of your environment. It energizes and relaxes at the same time. During meditation you are fully present physically, emotionally, and spiritually; in harmony with your surroundings. There is no expectation or plan. You are just *being*. Let intrusive thoughts pass through like a gentle breeze. You may sense spiritual guidance and wisdom during a meditation. Others may describe a blank place of quiet. It's a personal experience—yours and no one else's.

You might think you can't meditate because you are not able to shut off your brain. The goal of meditation is not to stop thoughts from forming. We can't really shut off our brain or empty the mind. The skill is in experiencing thoughts, but not letting them settle in. You notice the thought as it comes and let it pass, peacefully noting its presence, as it moves on through.

If you've never experienced a twenty minute meditation, it's hard to imagine what you do during all that time. You might assume it is boring, that you will become restless. At first, true, you may feel restless and bored. You may find your leg jumping or fingers tapping. A song or list will stick in your head. It gives you the opportunity to practice letting it go.

Again, the learning curve plays a part. You'll become comfortable staking out this time, and allowing your brain to rest. Like everything else worth having, it's worth working for. Persistence and practice will pay off.

Set a timer with a gentle alarm before you begin a meditation. Sit with the early restlessness. Persevere. The time will come when you achieve that undefinable space in your consciousness where exquisite peace resides. Once you settle in and learn the art, you will happily remain there until your timer chimes, signifying your return to the day ahead.

Research has been conducted on neuroplasticity—the change in brain structure resulting from experience. Emerging conclusions show a correlation between regular meditation practice and changes in brain structure. Researchers think meditation can be a vital factor in changing how the brain reacts to stress and pain. "With meditation, your brain is effectively being rewired," states Jessica Cassity in her online article "The Power of Mindfulness: Reshape Your Brain for Calm and Compassion." "The more your brain changes from meditation, the more you react to everyday life with that same sense of calm, compassion, and awareness."[7] This translates into less stress and better overall emotional and physical health.

Multiple brain-scan studies show changes in the density of tissue and an increase in gray matter in long term meditators. Some show results after only eight weeks of practice. In the coming years, I believe these studies will rewrite how we use mindfulness and meditation in conjunction with therapy and medicine.

In this section, we've covered information, insights, and incentives to prepare for a mindfulness practice. Take steps to manage stress and practice healthy life skills. Begin a lifestyle that includes radical self-care and a mindful life view!

HAPPINESS CALLING

__Part II__

Chapter 15:
Tools for Life's Journey

The following chapters are like a trip to Home Depot to stock a home repair toolbox. But you won't need to go to a megastore. You'll find one-stop shopping for emotional tools right here, a summary of techniques I've worked on with clients over the decades. What they learned increased their understanding and skill sets. Your toolbox will be stocked from the same inventory. I hope you'll take it along as you pursue your own path to happiness.

Earlier, we explored how childhood experiences and fears can manifest in our adult life. Now we'll review and address the resulting symptoms, and select tools to manage them. The intent is to provide a variety of tools and knowledge so you have options. You don't want to need the emotional equivalent of a regular screwdriver and only have a Phillips. You'll be prepared. You will have control. You will have choice.

Some tools will work for you, while others not so much. Take what's right for you, and fill your tool box. Carry it somewhere near your heart. Use it as needed, to develop and maintain the skills to sustain and nurture your growth.

This section is in alphabetical order so as not to ascribe value to one technique over the other. However, I do hope you'll keep Healthy Lifestyle in your toolbox. That section contains information about healthy eating, exercise, rest, and stress management. Adequate emotional self-care also includes taking care of your physical body. It's incongruent to work on emotional issues without also taking your health into consideration. By making healthy habits a priority, the rest of your growth comes easier.

***

Exercise 8: Let's take a moment to create a physical toolbox model. It doesn't have to be fancy (unless you want it to be). Get a paper bag or a teakwood box with velvet lining.

As you read on, take note of the gear and truths you think might be useful. Write them down on Post-it notes, and put them in your box. At the end you'll have a sense of direction about what information and tools you want to use. The box is a token of the mental toolbox you're creating for your continued journey. It will tangibly reinforce that you're equipped and ready to take on whatever comes. Being prepared gives you what? Control. And control gives you what? Choice.

Your needs will change as you proceed along your life path. Keep this book as a reference. If one tool seems to be losing its effectiveness, head to your dusty, dog-eared, doodled copy, and reread this section for a new tool, insight, or perspective.

Chapter 16:
Act as If

This tool places you one step ahead of where you actually are. With it, you claim the growth that is coming. It enhances self-esteem and helps to keep goals clear. You act like what you want to become.

As with every other growth curve, be patient with yourself. At first, as you begin to use this tool, you may feel embarrassed or self-conscious. Your self-talk may take on a tone of questioning your own grasp on reality. You might tell yourself you've become a walking stereotype. Take heart! Have faith. The discomfort will pass as you begin to enjoy the benefits.

Begin with acting as if you have the positive self-esteem you desire. Take good care of your body. Eat healthy food. Exercise. Manage stress. Walk with good posture. Speak positively about yourself and others. Have good eye contact and a firm handshake.

Beware of self-deprecating statements. While these can be seen as modest and humble, for the beginner they create a slippery slope to negative self-talk.

Practice accepting a compliment. Stand in the mirror and say, "Thank you," without tacking on, "It was nothing," or "I was just lucky." If you let kind words stick to you, they solidify into positive inner reflections.

If you aspire to be someone others can rely on, practice accountability. Use a day planner or the calendar on your phone. Make lists. Set up notifications to avoid missing deadlines and events—and birthdays and anniversaries. Do your tasks in a timely manner. Be on guard for self-sabotage. Keep your self-talk positive, and push through any desire to procrastinate. Don't be afraid to set goals.

If you're trying to be a more positive person, practice gratitude and mindfulness. Seek the good and focus on it. Say positive words, both to yourself and in affirming others. Stay away from complainers. Avoid those who are toxic to your growth. Choose affirming, positive, supportive friends and acquaintances.

Practice a pleasant look in front of a mirror. It doesn't have to be a constant, painted on grin, but a frequent natural smile does more than just turn up the corners of your mouth. It lifts your mood and encourages positive thoughts, as well as brightening someone else's day. You will find that positivity becomes cyclic, like so many other human behaviors. The more of it you put out there, the more you get back. In turn, the more positive you feel.

If you want to curb your alcohol intake or quit smoking cigarettes, avoid those activities. Stay out of bars, beer tents, and tobacco stores. Sit in nonsmoking areas. Order sparkling water or club soda with lime when dining out. Enjoy your fresh breath and clothes that don't stink of tobacco. Be honest with yourself about whether you need professional help in achieving these goals.

If you aspire to be a runner, do what runners do. Commit to a workout routine. Pay attention to the best time in your schedule to exercise. Then block it out on your calendar each day, as you would a dentist's appointment or a dinner date. Read books by successful runners. Enter 5k races and run-walk until it becomes a full run. Keep a log. Wear running gear, and buy good shoes. Frequent the running store to just hang out.

Dress the way you want to be perceived. Yes, it might sound stereotypical, but what you wear does reflect how you view yourself and how others see you. Claim where you are going. That includes the "uniform" of your goals.

If you hope to be a young professional in a conservative corporation, wear the pressed khakis. Join Toastmasters or Rotary. Choose social and leisure activities that will offer opportunities to meet mentors who'll help you advance.

At the same time, lay groundwork and do research. Learn about the businesses in your community. Study companies where you'd want to be employed. Be ready for that interview should the call come. Create the environment that will make that a reality.

If you want to be a folk singer, carry your guitar wherever you go. Dress in jean jacket and boots if that makes you feel more like the real thing. Sing at open mics. Visit listening rooms. Play ballads on the street. Study the styles of your favorite artists. Practice. Practice. Practice.

If you aspire to be a writer then write, write, and write. And read, read, read. Read books about writing by successful authors. Take classes, either online or at a local college. Attend writers' workshops and seminars. Attend readings and book signings. Keep a notebook in your back pocket or purse. If someone asks "Are you a writer?" say yes.

Be around people you admire. Get acquainted with them. Study them. Have mentors, people you look up to, who are further ahead on the path you pursue. This can be a formal relationship with meetings and coaching, or you might simply view someone as a mentor in your mind. You can refine your acting "as if" skills as you get to know them better. Use these folks as role models. Don't hesitate to ask them questions (but of course, don't make yourself such a pest that they avoid you). Listen to what they say, and put their advice into practice.

I had friends, a couple from my small, working-class hometown, who moved to the big city. They landed jobs that put them in the upper income brackets. Their new boss and his wife took them under their wings. With the boss's tutelage, they began with the basics, such as how to use all the forks and spoons at a fancy restaurant, and the etiquette of flying first class. My friends acted "as if" until they became comfortable in their new environment. I teased them that this couple, unofficial mentors, had taught them how to be rich.

One client described a woman she admired as "the kind of person who cuts her sandwiches in half diagonally." She said this woman was smart, poised, and socially comfortable — attributes my young client yearned to attain. We spent her next session exploring just what it was that kept *her* from cutting her sandwiches the same way, and how she would feel if she tried it. Her assignment for the next week was to act "as if" with the sandwich. It seemed silly to her at first, but it was a step forward in becoming a woman who cut her sandwiches diagonally, with all the implications tied to that simple act. She went on to change the way she dressed, her walk, her posture, and ended up with the job she desired. But it all started with a sandwich.

A vision board can be helpful when used with this "act as if" tool. It provides a visual picture of your future growth, an illustration of how you want your life to be. It gives you a focus to establish your short term and long term goals.

***

Exercise 9: It's time to get started on this vision board. There are no rules or specific guidelines in its creation other than that its presence, and the act of creating it, makes you feel positive and inspired. It visualizes your "as ifs" and snaps your self-care goals, future dreams, and what you want to be, into clearer focus. It's not all about formal goals, though. The most important factor is that it's energizing and empowering—and fun.

The materials are also up to you. It can be a poster, a cushioned board, a frame, your refrigerator—whatever you like. At first, think of a short term goal and a long term goal. Then pick out pictures, snippets of inspiration, bottle caps, feathers, bar coasters—whatever helps set your focus.

Remember when, earlier, we looked at the ideas and thoughts that didn't come to fruition? Now's the time to add them to your vision board, reframing each false beginning into a positive—a future aspiration you will one day be ready for. Add your gym pass, a page of your art class syllabus, and a picture from the gardening book. Now you have a reminder that you will achieve these, or similar goals someday.

When you look at your vision board or add to it, you're transported into the story of your future and how you will feel on that journey. Have fun with this pictorial of your intended path. Let your inner child play as you move forward together. Enjoy the good feelings as you anticipate what is to come.

Chapter 17:
Angels

We've spent time looking at how experiences and relationships shaped our world views—some negative, some positive. This chapter honors our angels, those who kept us safe, taught us truths, enhanced our strengths—and in some cases, helped us survive tough early years. These are the grandmas, the mentors, the teachers, and a best friend's dad. The angels in our life mirrored the good in us, and showed us a world beyond fear. They engendered hope. They saved us.

Who made a difference in your life? Who were you able to breathe with, to let down your guard? How old were you when you discovered there was life outside the fences placed around you by your family? When did you discover that maybe others saw you differently than you saw yourself? What event gave you the first hint not all families were like yours? When did you first grasp that not everyone lives in fear?

What you learned from your angels might have seemed as benign as discovering new things, or as life changing as rescuing you from toxicity and pain. An angel's work comes in different forms—a mechanic who let you tinker with engines, an aunt who taught you to roll out pie dough, a driver who took you to the library to get books about birds, or a heart who listened and heard your pain in the words you did not say.

A creative, intelligent client's family boxed her in, and kept her small. It wasn't intentional. They didn't know they held her back, frustrated her, and depressed her. They didn't seem to hear when she talked about dreams that took her away from their circle. They missed the clues of an exceptional brain yearning for sustenance.

She found her angel in a high school teacher. He taught freshman English. Brash and flamboyant, he carried an air of confidence she'd never seen. She let him read poems that she hadn't shared since fifth grade. He told her she was a good writer. He pushed her to do better—to do her best. In class, he expected open discussions about current topics. The students did outrageous things, like writing to Brian Epstein, inviting the Beatles to visit their small farming community. They tried chocolate covered ants and paté. They listened to rock music in class. They pretended they were the president's cabinet and solved the problems of the world.

In that small classroom, smelling of varnished wood and chalk dust, she and her classmates experienced the world. Some thought he was crazy. Others, pompous. Through my client's eyes, he was a mentor who taught her it was okay to dream - even encouraged it. He taught her to never be afraid to try to achieve her best. His favorite cliché was, "Reach for the top—if you don't make it, you'll at least end up in the middle." He lasted only a year at their small high school. But she would never see the world quite the same way again. Her eyes were open. She saw. She noticed now.

Another client had a similar awakening through a family friend. This woman was a part of her mother's circle that was the "village" that raised her. It was an unlikely group, brought together because their husbands and boyfriends were buddies. Church ladies, gamblers, drinkers, and thinkers. They became a mismatched set. They had each other's backs and, together, raised the gaggle of children they birthed. Though unique personalities, they still carried the stamp of small-town sisterhood.

Her mom's friend Mary had lived in the city. She had a career, husband, and four children. When my client was twelve, she'd gone with Mary to Chicago to see the stage production of *The Sound of Music*. The songs, the story, the experience changed my client. She'd left the theater wrapped in the glow of the evening. It opened her heart to the gift of music—all music. She could still enjoy Bobby Vee and the Drifters, but she also hungered for opera and classical. It opened the door to a lifelong passion. It also established a new coping skill. If things got tough, music healed. She would sit in the darkness and listen to *La Boheme* or *South Pacific*. It was her first experience with meditation. She just didn't know it yet.

Some angels arrive in adulthood, in the form of mentors, as we start to act "as if." They offer guidance and encouragement. Remember the client I referred to earlier—the one who admired the lady who cut her sandwich diagonally? That mentor was never aware of the impact she had. Yet she laid the groundwork for growth—a ribbon-cutting for the opening of a new chapter of a person's life.

Another client had a hands-on angel who coached and advised him every step of the way in his quest for academic success. The young man planned to get a job in the foundry of the plant in his small town after graduation. He had a strong back and big hands. He also had an IQ of 150. His mentor shared his thoughts about the young man's potential and options. He talked to the boy's family about scholarships that could make this quest a reality. The young man went to college. He didn't stop until he had a doctorate. His books on economics have changed the financial systems of the world. Years have passed. He never forgot his mentor. They still meet periodically to encourage each other, and brainstorm ideas.

For others, angels provide more than cultural awakening and dream building. They may offer shelter—actual survival. During my years of practice, victims of abuse and trauma sometimes found refuge at a grandparent's house, at a neighbor's whose door stayed open just in case, or at a friend's home whose family always had room for one more at the table. These angels may never have known the value of their meals, or rides, or hugs. The secrets may never have been told. They just instinctively responded to a vulnerable child.

We like to think all perpetrators of abuse are found out and punished. Luckily, most are. But the secret keepers, the good actors, the double-edged sword bearers can remain hidden behind shrouds of respectability and facades of the perfect family. It is for the children of these families, especially, that angels can make the difference between despair and survival.

A client found peace at Grandma's house every summer. Surrounded by love, he felt safe to explore and learn. He always had a story about something she'd taught him. She showed him how to love the little things around us. He smiled as he described a woman who worked seven days a week, smoked Tareyton cigarettes, and had the best legs in the family (according to Grandpa). They gardened and cooked what they harvested. He smiled as he remembered how she taught him service as they delivered cookies and meals to others, helped care for aging nuns at the mother house, and found shelter for travelers and animals in need. He learned to love music as she sat by his side playing piano duets. He learned how to write his name in cursive on a dark summer night with the desk light spotlighting his success.

The things he learned during those long summer days sustained him, comforted him, instilled a sureness that he could make it until the next summer arrived. He never shared with her about the abuse her daughter was capable of. He kept the secrets. She never knew the gifts she gave him. She just loved him and kept him safe.

***

Exercise 10: Who are/were your angels? Look at your timeline. Notice your rhythm. When did you feel afraid? When did you feel safe? When did you dream big? When did you discover new activities that made a difference? Use your journal or some loose leaf paper and make a list of the people who were there at those times. Write about your angels.

Have gratitude in your heart for the difference they made. Honor them. Thank them. If you can, really thank them. Let your angels know what they did for you! And then, think about ways you can pass it on to others.

Chapter 18:
Anger

What is anger? How do we express it? How and why should we avoid displaying it? At what cost? While discussing tools, we'll answer these questions and look at appropriate expressions. We'll also address those traumatized by rage and the cost of uncontrolled anger.

"I'm not mad."

"I'm just upset."

"It doesn't do any good to get angry."

"We never argue."

These are examples of our attempts to deny that we're angry.

Anger gets a bad rap. If we express or feel it, it's wrong. Especially for women. We fear judgment. Good people don't get angry. If we were raised in a "Don't talk, don't trust, and don't feel" home, it never seems safe to express negative feelings. We try to ignore and suppress anger. It gets pushed down somewhere deep. We bury it and turn away. If it's hidden and denied, it can't hurt us.

The only problem is that the premise is wrong. Hiding it does *hurt* us. And not just us.

Holding anger in can make you ill. It creates physiological stress that finds expression in headaches, gut aches, back pain, and elevated blood pressure, to name a few. Suppression of anger contributes to anxiety and depression. It's even been said that depression is anger turned inward.

It also hurts the target of your anger. You might not tell them, directly, that you're resentful, or the reason why. You don't yell or say mean words. But you're less engaged in the relationship, less spontaneous, less giving. Your interactions lack authentic warmth as you relate with passive disregard. You may forget to pick up the dry cleaning or "overlook" a lunch date, a birthday, or anniversary. If the relationship involves sex, you're going to be too tired, have a headache, or just not be in the mood.

The least fortunate victims of suppressed anger are those who become collateral damage. Holding in your rage makes you less tolerant and more irritable. The innocent checkout clerk isn't prepared for the tirade over bruised bananas. The dog who needed petting gets pushed away. Your little girl, spinning to show how her skirt twirls, loses her smile when tersely snapped at "Go change your clothes."

Collateral damage.

Negative feelings always find expression, no matter how much you deny their presence. Indirectly and passively, perhaps, but expressed just the same.

We all have tempers. It's a primordial, archetypal action inherent in all of us. After all, we come into the world screaming our outrage. Anger creates the terrible twos of toddlerhood. It's a normal human emotion.

Any time two people are together there's a potential for conflict. We can't live with another for long without their doing something frustrating. Sometimes it seems a daily challenge. Frustrations mount. We don't like to get enraged but despite ourselves, we do.

One reason some of us may be anger averse is we're still on a Mother Theresa track, working to be the best person in the world. If one is aspiring to sainthood, anger feels unacceptable and out of place. A saint never gets angry, right?

As growth continues, there will be increased self-acceptance. Perfection will not feel so necessary, either for Mother Theresa or for ourself. As we develop skills for appropriate expression, it will start to feel more comfortable to get riled up now and then, understanding that feeling the emotion does not equate to being a bad person.

Our own negative emotions are not the only anger we avoid. We also stay clear of others' fury. There are several reasons for this avoidance, but the bottom line is that anger makes us anxious and uncomfortable.

We might prefer to avoid others' anger if we were exposed to a high level of hostility as a child. Perhaps we were a victim or an observer of violent arguments, or a recipient of another's blows or screaming. Living through this trauma leaves us conflict averse. Any harsh tone or loud voice elicits the anxiety of the child within. The thought of getting yelled at, or being around one of those angry people, still creates anxiety.

This can also contribute to avoidance of our own anger. We might quake at the thought of being like our raging mother or father. Even appropriate expression of negative feelings carries shame. We fear we're like them.

We may also fear we'll lose control if we express anger. Rage can be a frightening emotion, especially if associated in our minds with injury or even death. So we continue the cycle of fear and suppression. The more we suppress it, the more it builds into a steep, toxic pile inside our brain. It strains and stretches until we get closer and closer to exploding with rage.

Finally it all comes tumbling out. As it spews out of our mouth, we scream all sorts of hurtful things we'll regret. How do we feel after? As you can guess, there is shame, self-blame, sickness—along with a horrible sort of relief that the pressure is gone. It convinces us once again that anger is bad. This supports the self-message that we are bad if we are angry, and that we can't control its expression. We can never let it happen again. And the cycle begins once more. Sadly, we get labeled as emotional abusers, and we live up to the reputation every time we get on this ride.

In the layers of avoidance, we may have forgotten how it feels to simply be angry. We have to work at it, and develop the skill. Anger is a strong emotion, but it is not a sin or a flaw. The task is to name it, respect its power, and learn how to manage its expression. Naming it and learning lessens fear and offers control. As insight increases, it becomes easier to identify how we feel, and what to do with those feelings.

So the next step is learning how to manage these feelings. That doesn't mean we become more effective stuffers! It means we learn to put space between impulses and feelings, words and behavior. With this skill in our toolbox, we become more confident in the ability to express anger appropriately.

We can manage our fear of anger and increase confidence in the ability to express it appropriately by creating a strong emotional IQ. Also known as emotional intelligence or emotional quotient (EQ), it is the ability to recognize, understand, and manage our emotions.

Impulses, thoughts, and feelings are our own. Private. The important factor is how we express these in words and behavior. That is where accountability comes in. The impulse might be to call someone every name in the book, and be in their face with spittle flying. But it's important to insert mental and emotional space between that impulse and the actual behavior response. We use emotional intelligence by pausing to assess and acknowledge how we're feeling, and consider how we want to express the feelings. During that pause, we're able to find a more civil way to get the point across. This offers up those lovely words—control and choice. As we gain more control and choice, the feelings become less frightening. We're then more comfortable in their expression.

Utilizing emotional IQ helps bring resolution to the conflict. We do not further enflame the heat and hurt. It increases the odds that our feelings will be heard and understood. Most of us just stop listening when we're yelled at or insulted, and communication becomes futile.

When working on boundaries, I talked briefly about the need to validate feelings. It's difficult to share your heart and your anger. You might argue that it does no good to tell someone how you feel, especially if you're angry. They will laugh at you, ignore you, or say you're wrong.

That may all be true. We can't predict another's response. The goal of expressing your feelings is not universal agreement and acceptance. It is not a means to always get your way, though speaking up increases the odds. The main function of sharing is to affirm to yourself that your feelings are valid. It strengthens you. You gain a shot of self-love when you say to yourself or others, "This is how I feel. My feelings are important, and they deserve to be heard. I feel this way for a reason, and I'm comfortable letting you know."

This may be outside your present comfort zone. You have perhaps never done it before, so as always, respect your learning curve. It helps to sit with your feelings a bit first. Write down your thoughts to sort out what made you angry. Then you are as ready as you will ever be. Stand straight, look the person in the eye and say, "I feel angry when you . . ." You will be amazed at the sense of relief. You are free now. You have been emotionally honest. In doing so, you have been self-affirming.

Use "I" words, as in the example above. Do not say, "You make me feel. . . ." Presenting it this way sounds accusatory, blaming. The other person will be put on the defensive before you even mention why you're angry. The other party in this equation is not *making* you feel any way. Your feelings are your response to her or him. They come from *you.*

At first, as you practice this skill, you might observe yourself getting overzealous in setting boundaries and expressing feelings. It happened in groups I facilitated. You begin by practicing how to say no, but it might initially come out sounding harsh or rude. There could even be expletives involved. It just feels so darned good to get all the stuffed stuff out, you might sound more aggressive than you intended!

Take heart. The pendulum swings in both directions. This pendulum has been resting in the red zone of the "yes person" for a long time. At first, it swings all the way to the other side. It will swing back. In the meantime, you'll get better at saying you're sorry—another important skill!

Before leaving this topic we have to return once more to the damage wrought by uncontrolled anger. This kind of rage may have wreaked havoc on your childhood, creating your nightmares and protective defenses. You may have grown up in an angry home, and you were the helpless child. Anger management problems can be another side of the same coin. You might be the kid who became the bully because you were bullied and shamed at home. You might be physically abusive to people you love because you were a victim or you saw your mother get hit. Anger begat anger, and you became that person yourself—the second generation abuser.

If so, I'll speak to you now. You seem to attack without remorse. Your victims are blind-sided by the explosion of rage. They weren't in your head the days before when the pile was starting to build. Your victims just see the rage. They don't know how sick you feel after you have hurt them deeply with words or physical pain. But you and I know that you care a great deal about your out-of-control rage.

The toughest challenge comes in accepting the cold reality that you choose to let go of your control every time you explode. It may not be consciously apparent at the time, but you *do* decide. You do not get off the hook with, "I can't help it." Yes, you can! Remember, *you* make the choice to let go of your control. You are accountable for the words that pass your lips and the fists that threaten or hit.

Get help from a therapist and an anger management group. With this support, you will deal with your own pain and shame. You will learn that the control comes in early recognition of red flags, signals that tell you things are starting to build. That's the point where you intervene. You'll learn how to express yourself appropriately by validating feelings and developing an emotional IQ. As you learn to express feelings as they come up, there will be less need for the stack of toxicity in your brain. Behavioral and cognitive skills will help you master your anger. In getting involved with a group, you'll also find you're not alone in your struggle.

Step up now. Tell someone this is a problem, and that you want to take responsibility for it. It will be the best day you have experienced in a long time.

Chapter 19:
Anxiety

E veryone experiences anxiety. It ranges from mild restlessness and edginess to full blown panic attacks. Mild anxiety can actually be helpful. It increases alertness. It's good for test taking and concentration on a task. It narrows and refines your focus, blocking out external stimuli, like noise and other attention detractors.

While mild anxiety is okay, increased levels create more challenges. In order to increase insight into them, this section offers tools for chronic anxiety, severe episodes, and panic attacks.

Severe anxiety or panic creates multiple physical symptoms such as racing heart, tightness in the chest, tingling, difficulty with swallowing, and sweating. It's accompanied by a dark feeling often described as a sense of impending doom. The first time you experience this level of anxiety it feels like you're dying. You fear for your life. You fear you're losing your mind.

I encouraged clients who experienced this to see their primary care physician for a physical exam first, to rule out any disease process. It's helpful to get medical assurance that it's not a symptom of a physical problem. This helps alleviate some anxiety right away, knowing it's not a life threatening illness.

You might still feel as though you're dying, but now you can assure yourself you're not. What is happening in your body is a normal physiological response to fear and danger. The chemicals coursing through your veins are for survival, a flight or fight response. They come in handy if you're hiking in the mountains, encounter a bear, and need to run like hell or climb a tree. Be thankful for it if you have to fight an assailant in the dark or lift a car off someone without even realizing you're doing it.

The problem with anxiety begins when the brain gets a wrong signal and begins screaming, "Danger, danger, danger," kicking the fight or flight system into action. Research shows that the amygdala starts things running amuck and misfires. But without an immediate physical threat in need of a superhuman response, you're suddenly stuck with an intense energy surge. It courses through your veins, creating all the symptoms that make up a panic attack. It feels like doom, chest crushing doom—until the chemicals dissipate. Then the feeling goes away.

Sometimes the source of the errant brain trigger is clear, like a fear of tight spaces, spiders, or falling. Often it takes putting pieces of the puzzle together in therapy to find the event that activated the fear response. Other times its cause is never determined. The best we can say is the brain randomly picked up a wrong signal without any apparent cause.

Once the trigger in the brain is sensitized, it can be more reactive for a while after an anxiety attack. During the time of increased sensitization, caffeine and other stimulants might cause mild anxiety. High humidity or a wave of dizziness may create a flutter. These go away once the trigger returns to a normal setting, but can be troubling when they occur.

No matter what the cause, here are two pieces of good news regarding panic attacks. One, no one ever died from an anxiety attack, and two, the episodes are self-limiting. The challenge is just getting through to the end of the episode.

I found when clients understood the function and physiology of their anxiety, they felt less afraid of the event itself. They learned to tell themselves, "It's only a feeling, and it will pass." Yes, it is a bad feeling, but it does pass.

One helpful tool, while in the midst of panic fear, is to ground yourself to the tangible things around you. Use your five senses. Touch the arm of a chair. Feel the fabric texture. Listen to birds sing. Watch trees sway in the breeze. Taste a strawberry or a pretzel. Smell coffee, cinnamon, or lemon. Your senses ground you to your environment and act as anchors when everything seems to be spinning.

Some find it helpful to get outside and move around, feeling movement and fresh air. Others feel better just sitting quietly or lying down until the episode passes.

Breath skills also aid in getting through spells. Breath focus not only slows stress signals, but it's another good grounding tool. Focusing on even, slow, deep breaths will also prevent hyperventilation, a physiological event that can lead to tingling around your mouth and extremities and lightheadedness. It's caused by rapid shallow breathing that can occur during an anxiety episode. This upsets the balance between oxygen and carbon dioxide in the blood, causing a rapid reduction in carbon dioxide. Breathing into cupped hands or a paper bag can restore the balance and the symptoms will abate.

These skills help decrease the intensity and length of the attack. In many cases, there are early warning signs. Some will feel a precursor symptom before the full panic attack hits, like a heart palpitation or feeling like there's a lump in your throat. Sometimes a dry mouth is the first sign. Recognizing early cues allows proactive intervention and can further decrease the intensity of the feelings.

But sometimes panic just comes out of thin air with no warning. It's difficult to be proactive in that case, but you can still use grounding techniques and breathe through the episode.

After experiencing an attack, you naturally don't look forward to another episode, so you often develop anticipatory anxiety. You fear that another attack is going to occur so you get anxious thinking about getting anxious. You start to think about the place, the situation, sounds, and temperature—everything about the environment where and when the anxiety occurred. The next time you plan to return to any or all of these, you become fearful you'll experience it again. This creates another layer of anxiety to battle.

If you were in a car when it hit, it may feel uncomfortable to think about getting back in the vehicle or taking the same route. If the anxiety occurred at the mall, it becomes challenging to go back. The anxiety tends to generalize to include the events or places where the event took place and all other factors surrounding it. You may start to avoid activities like driving or going to a store or a park. Try to manage this pre-anxiety to prevent it from generalizing. It's important to minimize its control over daily activities, as it can become very restrictive.

One client had an anxiety attack taking the "pod" to the top of the St. Louis Arch. The obvious trigger was the small, tight space. But my client remembered what he was wearing, the weather that day, the lunch he ate before arriving at the Arch. Over time, he became anxious on rainy, overcast cool days, never wore that shirt again, and developed an aversion to black bean soup. Eventually, even driving near St. Louis made him anxious. When we started our work together, his life had become restricted by the generalization of his anxiety to the point he rarely left the town he lived in. We took it step by step, untangled the fear and sorted it out, in order for him to regain control and freedom.

Another client had her first panic attack while taking a shower. The experience was so alarming, she began to dread each time she thought about getting back in the shower. She found herself avoiding the possibility of an attack by washing up rather than face the impending doom lurking behind the shower curtain. That anticipatory anxiety became as much a problem as did the panic in the shower.

We worked on self-calming skills, which included breathing techniques, imagery, and grounding along with positive self-talk about the experience. Over time, thinking about the shower no longer elicited fear, making the showering event itself less intense and easier to conquer. We worked on some practical solutions that gave her more control, like permission to shower with the curtain open. It didn't matter if the floor got a little wet. Slowly she was able to close the curtain a little at a time.

Sometimes the simplest solutions work.

Chapter 20:
Attitude

This section may seem like a review of our work on mindfulness. That's okay. It helps to have good things reinforced. Choosing the direction of your daily focus is one of your most useful tools. Most of us are capable of more happiness than we think. In most cases, it's attitude that limits how much good we see and how much we're able to enjoy life.

Think about the phrase, "I opened two gifts this morning— my eyes." If we start every morning with a mindful focus, we open ourselves to a day of beauty and miracles, spotting happy moments in places where we didn't expect them.

Have you ever stared at clouds or trees and seen a shape or a face? There's a term for that—pareidolia. Scientists have different theories as to why the brain operates this way and its psychological function. But it's a good illustration of where we choose to focus and the perspective we take from it.

I can stare at the chokeberry tree outside my living room window, and it becomes a hidden picture page from a children's magazine. If it's a season of sparse leaves, there is a spot that, if looked at one way, is a frowning woman. But after an eye-blink it's a smiling puppy. When the leaves are lush, that same spot might be James Brown's head or a fuzzy llama. Perspective! What's fun about this exercise is that I can flip my focus at will. Similar to visual illusion pictures, we get to choose what image we see.

It's the same with attitude. There's always more than one way to see a day, an event, or an image in a tree. Even at the worst of times, we can notice a singing bird or the smell of spring rain. There is no bad so bad it removes all good. The negative may cause a shadow or a veil. We may have to find a new way to look for the positive, but some good will remain. It will wait patiently to be discovered.

We start each day with a choice. There, on the edge of wakefulness, we can lament our poor sleep, muscle aches, the tasks that await us, and the irritating people we'll have to deal with. Or we can be thankful for the miracle of our heartbeat and awed by the dawn. With the latter, we anticipate the day's offerings, hopeful and optimistic that whatever comes is what we need. We will enjoy it, or find a use for it. As we discussed in Chapter 12, mindfulness allows us to give the day a chance. Yes, we may still have had a poor night's sleep, and our muscles may ache. But our choice to focus on the positive things around us that are just as real and tangible is what saves us from negativity.

Promise yourself even if challenges await, you will not miss the tiniest tease of happiness. Beauty can always be found, no matter what the circumstance. In the most hopeless of situations, Ann Frank wrote, "I don't think of all the misery but of the beauty that still remains."[8]

You determine how life events impact you. You can't stop bad things from happening. But you can control how they define you. Tough times never wipe out the good that exists, unless you let them.

Some people are born with seemingly insurmountable challenges, yet wind up doing incredible things. When misfortune, injury, or whatever we're dealt looks bleak and hopeless, you can become a bleak and hopeless person. Or these circumstances can lead to a deep acceptance of things you cannot change. Loss can leave you disabled or be a stepping stone. There's always some degree of choice. Sometimes it lies only in how to breathe. But that single act can save you.

We all have times of great challenge, but on an average day we don't. Most of us are regular people with regular problems and stressors. In this crazy, busy life, the smallest obstacles can loom large. Minor irritants become sources of frustration and stress. When we give into the negative we give it power and permission. Remember the old buzz phrase, "Don't sweat the small stuff," and the cultural add-on, "It's all small stuff"? Both are true most of the time.

Major crises and life traumas can be crippling. But, again, how many major crises do you have in an average day? I would guess that most of what sets us on edge, makes us angry, and drives stress is trivial stuff. This detritus of life sets us off. In the next day or week we won't remember why we were upset.

Take a minute and think about what made you tense today. What overwhelmed you? Now, look at this day as if it were your last hours on earth. Would you see things differently? I'm guessing the tepid coffee, the printer glitch, or the coworker's cough would not seem so important.

A friend of mine once shared a jewel of wisdom. When asked how he put up with all the crazy stress of his job and the unpredictability of his large family, he chuckled and said, "I just tell myself, if this were on a TV sitcom, I'd be laughing."

Perspective. Focus. Attitude. These define how we travel through life, and how much happiness we are able to grasp.

As another of my friends says, "Thoughts become things. Choose the good ones."

Each day holds good and bad. Where you plant your gaze determines how you'll feel at its end. On those rare occasions when you swear there's no good to be found, try Scarlet O'Hara's words from *Gone With the Wind* to get you through— "After all, tomorrow is another day."

And it will be a good one.

Chapter 21:
Communication

Relationship challenges usually arise from a web of circumstances. Various factors work together to bring about the perfect storm. But if I needed a one-word answer about what creates the most trouble, without hesitation I would point my finger at *faulty communication*. This culprit is in the middle of almost every emotional conflict. It might not be the only or greatest, but it's always there in the middle, stirring the fire. For that reason, this chapter explores tools to optimize the ability to be heard and to listen to others—the keys to healthy communication.

How can we improve communication to minimize its contribution to discord? We've already looked at the two major parts of constructive communication, emotional intelligence and validating feelings. If used effectively, these components foster honest and safe interactions. Emotional IQ offers the ability to listen to our partner without overreacting. It helps us avoid hurtful words and unnecessary anger that shuts down communication. In other words, think before you speak, and listen without judgment. If all involved in the conversation are respectful, it becomes less risky to share intimate feelings.

Other general guidelines also help you to be heard and understood. If you've taken a speech class or a corporate training session on communication skills, you've seen the model of the sender and the receiver. There are mechanisms in this model for checking and validating that the message you mean to send is received in the manner you intended.

This model is especially useful in couples work. Partners sit facing each other. They make eye contact, and have some form of physical touch. Partner one makes a feeling statement. Partner two listens and repeats what he's heard. Partner one then validates that that is what she said, or clarifies if the message wasn't heard as intended. The process is repeated until the message received matches the message sent. Only then does partner two initiate his own feeling statement. And the repeat-response process recurs.

At first, this checking for understanding seems tedious and unnatural, but after the partners hear some of the missed and lost messages, it becomes an important tool. Once mastered, it can be done less formally as a natural part of the conversation.

We often half-listen while doing something else, using the excuse of multitasking. We don't make eye contact or connect through touch. As we continue what we're doing, while the other person talks, there are a lot of "uh huhs" and "mmmms", but if asked to repeat what is being shared, it is unlikely we could.

Another communication block is if we're planning a response while the other person is talking. We sit there looking like an adult, but inside we're a wiggling, seat-bouncing child waiting for a chance to jump in. We miss the message as we keep reminding ourselves of what we want to say. Looking into each other's eyes and touching hands can help. But if our brains are already drafting a reply, we might as well not even be in the room. If we're not actively listening, our preconceptions can jump in and skew the message. We all know interrupting shuts down communication, but silently interrupting in your mind is just as damaging.

Remember the couple from Chapter 7, the wife who wanted to talk during her partner's football game? She was upset when he didn't respond the way they'd practiced in their session. While a good example of self-sabotage, it also illustrates half-listening on Todd's part. Sherrie chose a time when Todd wasn't ready to engage. When he half-listened, already thinking frustrated thoughts, he went into the dismissive "uh-huhs" and "mmm's". The communication was lost, and created more problems.

Touch and eye contact connect us. They set up the "wiring" for communications to travel through. When we minimize background noise and give each other our full attention, we set ourselves up for healthy communication. The connection was faulty for Todd and Sherrie, and the attempt failed.

Another roadblock is assuming you know what the other partner is thinking or feeling. When working with couples, I stayed alert for the phrases, "I think he feels," or "I'm sure she thinks." These statements are red flags. If we're guessing how someone is thinking or feeling, we're meandering down a path to failure and frustration. Based on these often-faulty assumptions, one partner might be sitting there thinking good thoughts while the other is saying to herself, "Bill's mad at me." With that seed planted, a winding road of unspoken assumption sets up defensiveness and hurt. Partner one doesn't have a clue anything is wrong. Then an argument erupts, and neither really knows why.

Be alert. If you hear yourself thinking for someone else, please "stop it." Step back and say, "I think you're feeling _____. Is that true?" You may be surprised and relieved at the answer you get. By taking the risk to ask, you can avert a conflict of your own creation.

Chapter 22:
Depression and Hope

There are many levels of feeling sad. Sometimes we have a bad day or a week of just being blue. We're out of sorts and want to just sleep through it.

Also, seasons of life or situations can cause us to be sad for a long time. When the situation is resolved, the depression slowly lifts.

Grief carries so much sorrow it buckles the knees, and we lie in a heap on the floor. Over time, we begin to put one foot in front of the other, and learn to walk again in a different world. We emerge with the strength to accept loss, and move forward. We're forever changed, yet able to seek happiness again.

These situations are emotionally crippling, for a time. But we do go on. The dark cloud lifts. Energy returns. We enjoy life once more.

We know we will get through a bad day, an upsetting situation, or grief—even though it will not initially seem that way. We don't want to feel these feelings, don't want to go through it, but, deep inside, we know it will get better. The task is to endure long enough to reach the other side.

But what about depression that comes for no apparent reason—that feels like it's forever? Life is good, filled with loving family and friends. There's no obvious reason to feel depressed. Yet a profound, pervasive sadness invades the soul.

The insidious joy killer that is clinical depression erases that secret sureness that it will resolve. It feels like a bottomless pit. There is no joy, peace, or hope.

This book provides many tools to manage and combat depression at most levels. But there are times in life, if symptoms are severe enough, that we just can't push ourselves to do what we need to do to feel better. At times like these, we may lack the psychic and physical energy to do even basic self-care or to seek support. Those negative streams of self-conversation return, darkening the mood even more. We can have a well-stocked toolbox, but if we can't pick it up, it's of little help.

This is an appropriate time to consult a therapist. It may also be a time when medication can be helpful. If you're depressed and don't have a counselor, contact your primary care physician. She will have assessment tools to help you understand your symptoms and will refer you to appropriate counseling. She might also prescribe a short term prescription, or refer you to a psychiatrist for a medication evaluation. Medication can help ease symptoms. Soon your energy and motivation will return. You take control of life once more, and use your toolbox to move forward.

If you ever reach a point where you feel lost, remember things always get better. Even if you can't believe it right then, trust that the words are true. Repeat them to yourself, over and over again. This will pass. If you feel hopeless, trust someone who has hope for you. If you have thoughts of self-harm, tell somebody. Let the people you trust lead you through the dark days. You'll feel the sun on your face again. I promise, that day will arrive.

Recovery from depression begins in glimmers caught at the corner of your eye. Healing starts with fleeting moments of light, like a glorious dash of hope. Slowly these glimmers turn into moments of peace, then hours of lightness. Eventually entire days will pass free of shadow. Happiness will once again have its way with you. Just have hope. It will always get better.

The hope you hold, or rely on from others, during tough times is crucial to recovery. It's also vitally important in a counseling relationship. Research on the effectiveness of therapy indicates that the number one variable that predicts success is the therapist's ability to engender hope.

Many clients walked through my door without hope, crippled by bone crushing emotional blows. In those times, my first task was to communicate unequivocal, unwavering faith that they could get through the pain. I gave them my hope, as a lifeline, until they found their own.

If you find yourself in the midst of a crisis, use self-talk to repeat over and over, "It will get better. It always gets better." The acuteness of the crisis will pass, and you will get your bearings back. You will feel tangible hope once more.

The return to strength takes time. At first it's a matter of holding on and letting others carry you through. But you'll find your legs again, and stand strong to continue the journey.

Time really does heal wounds. Humans are adaptive creatures. No matter the loss or pain, the severity of depression or anxiety, time passes. The mind and heart assimilate changes. The experience becomes part of who you are. It might profoundly change you, but there will be joy again.

These words also apply if the loss is your own health. Physical changes can create feelings of deep loss. You experience grief. Any event that changes life in such a way that you will never be exactly the same again causes grief. You need to trust your body and brain to help process the new circumstances, and come to a new peace and happiness.

Respect and honor the time it takes. And always hold on to hope.

Chapter 23:
Forgiveness

Earlier we looked at the importance of acknowledging old hurts. Validating these feelings is valuable in the healing of childhood wounds.

The next step is exploring who you have forgiven and what you still carry. Whether from the past or the here and now, carrying unforgiven anger is a burden. You can hold on to hurt until it becomes emotionally and spiritually toxic. Revengeful thoughts and acts might fuel your days. These pollute and create emotional and physical stress. When you realize the toll this burden takes, you will know it is time to forgive.

There are layers of forgiveness. First, accept that you have been deeply wounded. Next, acknowledge that you're angry and hurt. Then spend time with the burden of anger over the long term, and assess its effect. Think about why you're reluctant to forgive. What makes it so hard to let go of the pain? See the cost. Most times, you find the anger and vengeful thoughts are hurting you more than the other person. It's time to let go.

Once you make a conscious decision to forgive another, it does not just automatically happen. There are no magic forgiveness wands. It is a choice you make to move on from the pain. In doing so, you will find you have to re-immerse yourself into the hurt, for a time. Only then, once you have looked it square in the eye, named it, and stood up to it, can you purposefully turn away.

You forgive, but you do not forget. It's impossible to erase life experiences from the brain. What has passed is ingrained and woven into who you are. You can't pull one string out of your life's weaving. It's there. It happened. But by choosing forgiveness, you stop nurturing the memories, the feelings, and the pain. You lay it down and let it go. You walk away, free of the toxicity it carried.

Forgiveness eases the soul, but it takes time to get there. Deciding to forgive is the first step. I've heard it compared to giving someone an expensive gift that you charge on a credit card. The recipient of the gift of forgiveness gets to enjoy it immediately, while you have to take time to pay the debt of the decision. That debt comes in the form of soul-searching self-honesty and the struggle of letting go.

Forgiveness might lead to the resumption of a relationship. It might not. It doesn't necessarily imply that you will love or trust the person again. The damage may be irreparable. Letting go of pain makes you stronger, and able to make that decision objectively. It's a choice you get to make.

***

Exercise 11: This assignment provides a guided imagery tool for forgiveness. Pick the person or persons you want to pardon.

Envision all the memories of hurt and pain laid out on the dining room table. They're in full view for all to see. That table hasn't been cleaned off in a long time. Every time you walk by you pick up each memory and fuel the flame.

"Oh when he did this he was such a jerk. I will never forgive him for. . . ."

"If she hadn't lied to me we could still be friends, but now. . . ."

"My life was ruined when she left me."

You stir up the anger and hurt. You hold on tight, letting the poison seep in through the pores of your skin and the air you breathe. You fan the fire every day with revengeful thoughts and clenched fists.

Then comes the decision to forgive. On that day, you set a box on the dining room table. Look at all the pain spread out on the table one more time. Then neatly place each betrayal in the box. When you've cleared the table, put the lid on the box and tie it up with ribbon. Let tears fall and feelings flow.

Take the box to the hall closet, and put it on the shelf above the coats, alongside stocking caps and plaid wool scarves, seasonal decorations, and outgrown clothes.

Now shut the door. Stand there for a minute. Sigh a long sigh. Take a deep breath, and walk away from that closet that now holds all the pain. Dust and polish the now empty dining room table. Add a nice runner and a vase of spring flowers. It's fresh and clean now, ready to be used for better things than holding anger and pain.

Each time you open the closet, you might glance up at the box. You may hold in your breath and experience a pinprick of the old hurt. You say, "Oh, I remember all that from my past." But you won't take it down. It's put away. The pinprick will fade. You close the closet door and go on with your day.

***

It's been said that when you forgive you give up the right to keep treating someone badly. The cleansing of forgiveness heals the mean, self-righteous spirit of revenge. It's not needed any longer. You're free in a whole new way thanks to this conscious act of forgiveness.

This exercise can also be applied to yourself. As self-awareness increases, you may find there are things you have never forgiven yourself for. Find where you keep your secret stash of self-blame for only you to see, and go through the same exercise. Pick it up, examine it, and then put it away.

Chapter 24:
Generosity

As self-awareness increases, we're more likely to fine-tune our moral compass. In this process, we become more emotionally generous. This section offers truths that will be helpful on this quest.

I hold a deep faith that humans are essentially good. We want to be that way. We feel our best when we are. In the movie *Starman*, Jeff Bridges plays a lovable nineteen-eighties alien. He tells his earthly sidekick that his favorite thing about us humans is that we're at our best when things are at their worst.

I've seen this fictional wisdom play out over and over. In the midst of personal or communal tragedies, we experience primal moments of goodness. During these times, we feel vulnerable and raw. We rise up with open and responsive hearts. It is involuntary, like a heartbeat. We huddle, and take care of one another.

In everyday life, a commitment to essential goodness isn't as easy. We can be weak, lazy, easily influenced, and sometimes attracted to the dark side. Society, unwittingly, lures us.

"If it feels good, do it."

"Every man for himself."

"It's a dog-eat-dog world."

"Take what's there for the taking."

Following these philosophies may leave us empty and disconnected. They reinforce loneliness and negativity, and leave us cynical. Life lacks meaning. Rather than working to be our best, we roll down the slippery slope of apathy, becoming fatalistic on the way down.

In getting to know ourselves, we develop a level of self-honesty about our strengths and challenges. We're aware of the good and the bad in us, without internal blind spots. It is then that we make conscious choices that define how we live. In doing so, we face the challenges. We make an objective decision to live the life Emerson spoke of.

You will not choose the high ground every time. You will struggle. There will be days you won't want to bother. This is one area where the act "as if" tool can be useful. If you want to be a generous person you need to act like a generous person. Force yourself until there is a force in you. For example, you may not, naturally, want to listen deeply to another's story. But force yourself to sit still and actively listen. It is a practice to be learned, but you know it's worth the effort.

You always feel better when you are kind. You get better at kindness, and the force develops as you make yourself do the hard, dirty work of small, loving acts. Take the trash out for your spouse. Let that merging driver in with a wave and a smile. Take the grocery cart to the cart parking spot. Take someone else's, too, while you're at it. Leave a big tip. Pick up the litter someone else left in the park. Tell the neighbor with the beautiful flower garden that walking by her house makes you feel happy. Every kind act imprints on your heart until generosity is your natural choice, more often than not.

You have the freedom to explore undiscovered parts of yourself, good and bad. Finding balance requires the courage to look. There will be days when you are just not feeling it. On those days force yourself to do, at least, one kind act. It won't always be clean and pretty. Your heart may not be in it. Do it anyway. Your inner grump will grumble, but put a bow on the kindness, and it will clean up nice just the same. As a result, you will feel better, and the recipient of your kindness will feel blessed by your grudging act of emotional generosity.

An old Cherokee legend speaks to these struggles. A chief tells his grandson the story of two wolves battling inside each of us, one good and one evil. His grandson asks which one wins. The old Chief tells him the wolf that wins is the one we feed.

Which one will you feed?

Good deeds and actions truly do repay you. Remember "Do unto others as you would have them do unto you" and "What goes around, comes around"? It's true. Yes, you do reap what you sow.

A decision to live an honorable life is in itself fulfilling and rewarding. You'll slip. It's inevitable. But if you strive to be emotionally generous and treat others well, more often than not the benefit will be a whole new level of joy and contentment.

Be sensitive to the reality that you don't know what burden another human being carries. Smile at the checkout clerk who never smiles. Her sadness may be sourced in some abuse unknown to her customers. Hold the door for the cranky, old lady whose children may never visit or call. Wave at the scowling, harried driver whose wife may be dying of cancer.

Be open to the briefest opportunities for connection—a smile, a wave, or holding a door. Some will come at the most unexpected times. Think of a crowded elevator. We all stand there, looking down or straight ahead, our personal space threatened. Stiff and unsmiling, we wait in silence until the door, mercifully, opens to our floor. But there are those moments when someone races up as the door is closing. Some brave soul sticks a foot in the door to hold it open. There's a communal cheer for the runner to get there before the door shuts on the shoe. Everybody's laughing and talking. It's a connecting moment. For that seemingly inconsequential time we let down our defenses. We become one. The moment will pass, and we will go on our way. But it leaves us smiling. The tribe of elevator people helped, maybe saved the day. We feel warmer and softer in the afterglow.

Another tool that helps us to remain mindful of how we impact others is the Thumper philosophy. Remember the cute little rabbit in *Bambi* and the wisdom imparted by his mother? What does she tell her little bunny son? "If you don't have something good to say, don't say nothin' at all." Amen.

Those words are also useful as a reminder to avoid gossip. Remember, if someone is talking to you about someone else, he or she is likely gossiping to someone else about you. This is another place where using your emotional IQ comes in handy. As you step back, you can discern—is this a conversation of concern or gossip? From there, you decide whether or not to participate.

Also, be aware of little white lies you may tell. Examine where they come from. Are you trying to make yourself sound better than you really are? If so, use them as a constructive guideline to live up to those subtle untruths. Then, stop telling them. If you do, acknowledge them and apologize. This level of emotional transparency keeps you accountable and helps build trust.

We can be critical and judgmental creatures. Often we're unaware of how deeply our words or actions can hurt. As we are kinder to ourselves, our sensitivity to others increases. Remember, the more accepting and loving of ourselves, the more accepting and loving we are toward others. This expands beyond your intimates outward to those you meet incidentally on your journey.

Think of the good you've done and mistakes you've made. There's a lot to feel happy about, but there are also regrets that come to mind. If you're like me, it is the times you failed to be emotionally generous that still bring tears. It is the thoughtless rudeness or passive disregard for others on bad days. The calls not made, the time not spent, the times I was too busy to listen.

So call your mom. Leave a note of appreciation for your roommate. Hug your friend. Tell the postman you appreciate his hard work. Watch the little girl next door as she shows you her puppy's trick.

Life is precious. Love is precious. Don't let those intended acts of kindness collect dust in the vault of good intentions, where they moulder into regrets. Choose to be generous with your heart and your time.

Chapter 25:
Health

I fancy myself an expert on wellness. Others may say "fanatic," but "expert" is a good reframe. You'll find truths and tools to support your commitment to radical self-care in this section.

A healthy lifestyle is an integral part of emotional and spiritual health. When the body feels good we're much more likely to be in good spirits. It's easier to maintain a positive attitude. There's energy to venture into new realms of self-discovery.

The body seeks a healthy balance called homeostasis. We are either a misfiring engine, in need of tuneup, or a smooth-running machine that functions at peak performance. When living a healthy life style, we choose to pursue the latter. There's no magic in this and no guarantees. But pursuing this path increases the odds for good health. When challenges do come, the body's stronger and more resilient.

I conducted many wellness workshops as a part of my therapy practice. Most focused on women over fifty, but the information applies to all ages and genders. I taught the basics of nutrition, exercise, and stress management, in an enriching environment.

In the first session, while we ate healthy apple walnut muffins with lemon water and herbal tea, I presented the hard facts on what refined sugar and high-fructose corn syrup do to insulin levels, hormones, and health. I outed processed food (most anything in a box) and artificial additives. We explored the benefits of plant-based eating and the value of organic meats and dairy. Each participant completed an assessment of her own eating habits, and we worked on a plan. It wasn't a one-size-fits-all diet that required military-like commitment and deprivation. It tailored a healthy food guide to their personal likes and dislikes.

Workout clothes were required for the second session. On arrival, each participant received a yoga mat, light dumbbells, and a baseball cap. We moved through light cardio exercises and hand weight routines. I shared research about the dangers of a sedentary life. We looked at stress, depression, arthritis, diabetes, heart disease, and decreased brain function—just a few of the issues related to lack of exercise.

I didn't intend to make them body builders or marathon runners, but to alert and energize them to move each day, even for a ten minute walk. There was a picture in their reading material from the *Growing Bolder* website of an eighty-year-old woman balancing parallel on gymnastic bars. The header said, "If you rest, you rust." That just about says it all.

I stressed the importance of casual movement, as well as an exercise plan. There are studies of global Blue Zones where people tend to live healthier, longer lives. These indicate one unique, common factor: people who live there are less sedentary than other populations. They're more naturally active—walking and bicycling for transportation, working, and gardening. Their diet is also more plant based.

In the case of my fifty-plus group, I wanted them to know exercise is for everyone. One of my ladies had a bad back and was scheduled for surgery. Another had a rotator cuff shoulder injury and could barely raise her arm. I showed them exercises adjusted to their limitations. We drank berry smoothies, ate protein bars, and laughed a lot.

Self-care and mindfulness were the topics for the third and final session. We had candles, a small water fountain from my office, and soothing music. We went through guided imagery and yoga stretches. I wanted them to experience complete relaxation.

While my workshops were for the over-fifty group, I preached wellness to all my clients. It's important for all of us to understand the control and choice we have regarding our health. I'm thankful when I see young career people or crazy-busy dads and moms who take the time to prioritize their wellness. Like most habits, it's easier to keep going, as you age, if you started in your youth.

But it's better to start late than not at all. Sadly, some folks think themselves into old age. Preconceived ideas influence self-talk as birthdays pass, and we experience the first creaky knee or crêped skin. As in so many other areas, self-talk shapes our attitudes as we grow older. As the attitude goes, so goes the body, mind, and soul. That's true at any age, but stakes grow higher as birthdays pass.

Some of us assume we will get sick, take a gazillion prescriptions, and get swallowed up in a drug plan donut hole. We have an ache, so we quit moving. As we quit moving, we ache more. We get depressed because we sit around all day, and ache even more. We quit cooking and socializing, golfing and gardening. We forget that we were created to be healthy. We forget we have control and choice.

Our bodies work hard to stay in balance, but we have to do our part. Aging doesn't have to mean illness or disability. No one's going to live forever, but why not live your best until then? It's exhilarating to help others grasp that, and see them get excited again.

If a serious illness does hit, a strong immune system is ready to fight. The odds of recovery are better. Sometimes we have to learn to live with a chronic disease, or battle a life-threatening illness. If we have a strong body and a positive attitude in place, it increases our ability to cope and recover.

One woman I know very well developed severe osteoarthritis. For years she ignored her symptoms. Five years ago she started to have painful back spasms that limited her activities. She lived on ibuprofen and a heating pad. She quit exercising. Her pain not only persisted, but worsened. She felt debilitated and depressed. She felt old.

After MRIs, bone scans, and physical therapy, she heard all kinds of foreboding words. The recommended treatment plan was pain management with pain medication and muscle relaxers. She said no. That was not going to work for her.

With the approval of her family doctor, she chose to pursue a wellness-based approach to health—therapeutic massage, yoga, and spinal manipulation. The chiropractic practice she chose offered a program of nutrition and stress management. She already ate relatively healthily, but now became a soldier for clean eating.

She's since become more energetic and active, and gone back to regular exercise. She'll never run again, but she is a wicked walker. She's not going to bench press one hundred pounds, but she works out with lighter weights. She practices yoga. She bicycles. She's taken up kayaking and tried tap dancing. She marches in parades with a bunch of fun and zany women. She enjoys playing with her grandkids. She's not depressed. She's not debilitated. She's not old. She's even written a book.

That woman is me.

I consider myself one of many success stories. If the major challenge of serious illness comes, I'm prepared for the battle.

The path to health doesn't have to be dramatic or miraculous. It's a simple prescription. Keep moving. Put one foot in front of the other, and be mindful of the food you eat. Mix that with equal parts of good attitude and managed stress. It makes a clear and consistent difference in how you feel.

No matter your age, move your body most days. Do light cardio, resistance, and stretching activities. Attend a yoga or tai chi class. Get out and do things you enjoy. Take a class. Start a salad or herb garden. Walk your dog. Take a child to the park. Listen to music. Dance. And, yes, do the little things. Take the stairs instead of the elevator. Park farther out in the grocery store lot.

Avoid packaged food if it has more than five ingredients. Be able to pronounce all of them. Eat only healthy fat, and limit processed sugar and other white carbohydrates. Eat fresh whole foods—organic, if possible. Check out the Environmental Working Group's Dirty Dozen and Clean Fifteen fruits and vegetables for guidance. Become a regular at farmers' markets. Get to know the farmers and gardeners. You not only learn the source of your food, but join a tribe of conscious, thoughtful humans.

This kind of health plan is not about deprivation or never eating a certain food again. It's about being mindful of what you put in your mouth, and intentionally honoring your body with proper fuel to maintain optimal performance.

A friend of mine is going through cancer treatment. Her goal is to eat healthy eighty-percent of the time. The other twenty percent, if she wants potato chips or a piece of pie, she eats it. You may find the desire comes less often the longer you eat clean food. But when the yen strikes, go ahead and indulge. (Just use moderation!)

It's also important to get good sleep. The brain needs rest. By the end of the day, if it had a computer screen, it would show too many tabs open. Just like that computer, the brain needs to reformat in order to put all the files in their proper place. It has to process the day and all the information taken in. Meditation and quiet time offer one level of rest, but sleep provides the complete shutdown. This relieves the brain of the constant stimuli of the day.

For these reasons, sleep hygiene is another essential to optimal health and stress management. There are multiple resources available to help you have good rest. Some tips: consistent bedtime and waking hours, staying away from electronics and screens for the hour prior to sleep, and avoiding stimulants like caffeine later in the day. It's also helpful to sleep in a cool, dark room.

Establish a bedtime ritual. If you have a cup of herbal tea while reading a calming book for your last hour of wakefulness, then wash your face and brush your teeth before you get into bed, the brain associates these activities with "It's time to go to sleep." This routine sets in motion the slow preparatory action that sets your brain up for a good night's nap.

If you have insomnia, before resorting to medication try these options to establish your best sleep pattern. Most times, sleep can be improved by these self-care techniques.

I was a nurse for many years. I believe in conventional medicine. There are some things only it can treat. But we also need to be aware of effective alternative options and use them when appropriate. Be an active member of your own health team. Choose well!

Chapter 26:
Journaling

Writing helps us discover what we feel. Journaling can be a daily ritual, but it's also a tool for dealing with life events as they come. Try it. You'll grow to love it. The act of putting pen to paper can be an adventure. You never know what feelings will show themselves. It's like cream that rises to the top of raw milk. You wait for it to gather, then skim it off the top and make something good out of it.

Putting thoughts and feelings to paper is another means of externalizing feelings. It purges. If you're stuffed with feelings, journaling can be cathartic. It's like hitting the punching bag for twenty minutes or running five miles. Instead of pounding those feelings into the punches or the pavement, you fling them onto the paper.

Here are some journal ideas to add to your toolbox.

The Journal Letter: We all have unfinished business in life and words we wish we'd said. It may be to the ex-partner, parents, friend or boss. Maybe there are words that are difficult to say to yourself. You might be reluctant to let loose of what you hold. If someone died you're left with the bitter taste of the unsaid. The words are left with nowhere to go, forever unexpressed.

Journaling can help you find peace in these situations. Whether it's unexpressed anger and hurt, apology or forgiveness, the journal letter gets it outside of you. It affords you the closure you need to let it go.

These letters need not be written with the intention of sending them. This is for you, not anyone else. Sit down and write every word from your gut. Make it brutal in its honesty. Get it out.

If the letter is the end of the communication, honor your words. Have a ceremony, a rite of passage, and let go the burden. Get a fire-safe dish or go outside to the sidewalk. Light the edge of the paper with the flame of a candle. Lay it down and watch it burn. When it simmers to ash it's a thing of the past, no longer able to weigh on your soul.

Some letters could begin a path to gentle confrontation. They might become first, second, third drafts of a missive you will eventually really send, in order to be finally free. If that need is there, it will evolve with the journaling. Keep rewriting until the words are polished, burnished from being so tight up against one another that they shine.

Journaling for Discovery: Journaling helps you figure out what you're feeling. It's for those times when you're just out of sorts. Looking back over the day, you can't quite pinpoint what put you off kilter.

Start by writing the events of the last twenty-four hours. First it's like newspaper reporting, but soon it becomes connected to feelings you didn't realize were there. Journaling becomes the pen and paper equivalent of retracing your steps searching for lost keys. Just as you find the keys in the couch cushion or under a stack of mail, you'll find the beginning of your foul mood tucked inside a coworker's frown or the foreboding shadow of the afternoon sun.

Once you understand, you own the feeling. Only then can you do something about it, and work your way back to a better mood.

Gratitude or Affirmation Journal: Both these tools deal with the positive. The subtle difference is the focus. Carry these journals with you at all times. The little sixty-nine cent spiral notebook is perfect. It fits in a pocket or purse. You can keep them separate or combine them into a positivity journal. You can even keep them in the Notes app in your cell phone.

The gratitude journal is an exercise in mindfulness, setting the spotlight on the beauty of every minute. It's a means of returning your heart to the positive, reminding you no matter what stress or pain you face, blessings and beauty still abound.

An affirmation journal is a self-esteem exercise. It turns your attention to good things about you and your life. It's a tool to counteract that stream of negative self-talk we addressed earlier. It's positive self-talk put in writing.

Keep these journals close at hand. Use them when you're out and about. If you run across a gratitude moment or you've done something that deserves a self-compliment, write it down. It's also handy to have these nearby when you feel like nothing is going right, or in case of a self-attack of negativity. Pull that book out, wave it, and say, "I beg your pardon, but my little book says different."

Dream Journals: Years ago my mentor told me that the heart of therapeutic material is in early memories and recent dreams. We've already dealt with the value of insight into early memories. But what about dreams?

I'm not a guru of dream interpretation, or an expert in Jung's collective unconscious, but I respect the nighttime workings of the mind. You will likely notice, as you spend more waking hours processing feelings and memories, your dream life will increase. It's as though all your levels of consciousness work as a team.

You might begin to dream of events from your past of which you had little or no consciously accessible memory.

Symbolic dreams of fears and insecurities could become a regular occurrence. At first you might be frightened by these and be reluctant to examine them. Stay with them, though. They're crumbs left on the path to help you find the way.

A thirty-year-old client was working on relationship issues with her mother. She was dealing with fears that kept her from letting go and transitioning to a healthier adult-adult relationship. She began to have dreams of rescuing her mother from a flooded house and others about being surrounded by water. We explored water as symbolic of cleansing and new beginnings. Through the process, she realized she was beginning to heal. The dreams provided the initial unconscious evidence of letting go. From there, she was able to take steps forward in her therapy.

Keep a notepad at your bedside. If you wake in the night from a dream, jot down enough to assure you'll remember the content the next morning. If your first waking feeling is sorrow or anger, follow the crumbs back to the night's dreamscape. Some dreams won't make sense at first, taking bizarre twists and turns, but may become clear later. Others will smack you in the face with revelation and "aha" moments.

Art Journaling: If you like to draw, this type of journal can be a pleasant addition to your toolbox. Use whatever medium you like. It's helpful to have your work gathered in one place — a notepad, book or binder. Let it tell your story.

As with other forms of journaling, you'll discover what there is to find. Sometimes insights come directly from your work. Others come in the back door.

A client struggled with father issues from his childhood. He began an art journal in a favorite book of verse, creating colored pencil representations of his challenges. He selected pages inscribed with meaningful verses related to his drawings. It was a tool for him to express himself and reconnect with a hobby he loved. He looked forward to his time each day.

Then one week he reported struggles. He found himself avoiding the art journal. He became aware he was whispering negative self-talk that he was wasting time. We discovered these words were his father's. As a child, if he was doing an activity that Dad deemed "idle work," he was admonished and assigned a list of chores. He was repeating this pattern as his adult self.

This revelation gave him the courage to challenge the self-talk. At the same time he was able to work on critical father issues. In a couple weeks he was back enjoying his journal time.

The Brain Binge: In 2013, an EF4 tornado devastated a small town in Illinois. Several hundred structures were destroyed. A sizable portion of the town was gone in minutes. The loss of life was miraculously small, but a large part of the population had only seconds to find shelter. The tornado occurred ten miles from my office.

The victims were overloaded. In response to trauma, the brain tries to make sense of what happened by playing the scenes over and over. It creates an obsessive loop of the traumatic event. At the same time, the practical issues of shelter, food and clothing, and insurance adjustors required attention.

After crisis debriefing and trauma processing, the task of putting lives back together took priority. It was difficult for the victims to face the damage and contemplate what to do to recover. We tried to provide a safe environment for these vulnerable folks who felt as if they would never feel safe again.

There may have been trauma in your life also. If so, you know what it's like to be overwhelmed. Like the victims of the tornado, you may have found yourself assaulted by memories and feelings, as the brain tried to make sense of it all. It becomes like a computer virus. Your mind has difficulty functioning at that level. It wants to just shut down. It is these times that the brain binge journal is helpful.

It's a way to dump the contents of your head onto paper. Sit down with a notebook. Lean your forehead on your non-writing hand, and let a direct connection to your writing hand develop. Let the information race down that connector and out your hand. You're not making an organized list. Your hand is merely a vehicle for the export of material. Free write. Write until nothing's left to write. Then shut the notebook.

Resist the desire to read what you wrote. That's for another time. Later, sit down with the brain binge notebook and a new notebook. Now you can read what you wrote. With highlighters, mark the feelings. Then look at what's left.

Take the task items and put them in the new notebook. This will become your to-do book. Create a short list for each day of the next week, leaving a couple of blank spaces on the list for things that may come up. Work only from the to-do book. Go day by day. Do not look ahead to the next day. Only attend to one twenty-four-hour period at a time. This helps you regain a sense of control.

Whenever you feel your mind racing or you lie in bed at night making lists, go back to your brain binge book. Start the process again.

Begin to journal about those highlighted feelings when you're ready.

Worry Time: Worry time is not, technically, journaling, but it does require writing.

Worry can be a daily challenge. If you're prone to this burdensome battle, you're aware that the source can be as benign as an upcoming family dinner or as out of your control as the latest global crisis.

We all worry. It's a matter of degree that makes it a challenge for some and not for others.

Perhaps you are one who manages your worry and doesn't have this daily battle. But if not, you may be the one who envies that friend who says he or she isn't worried, "I'll worry about it if it happens," or "I can't change it anyway so why worry?" And they really mean it. Are they your heroes?

I understand, since I've done my share of worrying. But I've learned that there's always something to worry about. I was taught not to get too excited about an upcoming event because I might get disappointed. That translated into worrying even about the good things. When I got tickets to see the Beatles, they sat housed in the fire-safe, important-papers tin until the concert. I would alternate my worry between impending nuclear proliferation and the reliability of the fireproof tin. I made myself sick in the waiting, sure that I would never see the Beatles.

Worry in any form robs you of joy and relaxation, creating a chronic undercurrent of tension and stress. You never really put it aside.

I hope the following instructions will help you take control of your worrying. It won't make you worry free. You're probably not going to become the happy-go-lucky, laid-back person of your dreams. But you'll be able to manage your worry more effectively, and keep it from impinging on your ability to enjoy life.

My prescription is "worry time." As I said, this tool is not designed to cure your worry, but to help you organize and manage it. Honor the function of worry and accept that you are a worrier. You worry for a reason. The more important challenge is how to control it so it doesn't control you.

Get your journal or another inexpensive notebook for your worry time. Start with a twice-daily schedule. Plan on designating a specific time for each session. Do this every day, at first, around the same time. Designate a spot as your worry space. Set a timer. Start with ten minutes, but slowly increase to thirty minutes as you begin to see the benefit. Then write down the things you're worrying about today.

Is it your health, a phone call you have to make, a deadline at work that is upsetting your stomach? Whatever it is, put it to paper. Don't think about arranging the worries in a hierarchical order. No worry is more important than another. They all affect you physiologically the same.

Now look at your list and spend a few minutes on each entry. Wring your hands, pace, cry, pray, or wail. Express whatever feelings you have. But when the alarm chimes, you're done. It's the end of that session.

The rest of the day, if a worry pops into your head, address it only by jotting it down in your worry book. Trust that it will be attended to at the next scheduled worry time.

In doing so, you honor your worry, but you take control. This is a simple exercise, but if you remain faithful, it is extremely effective. With practice, you will be able to put worries aside once they're in the book. Rather than your day being burdened by chronic worry, it's condensed into two specific times. The rest of your day is worry-free.

This tool helps to manage an issue that otherwise can leave you overwhelmed. You become confident that when the appropriate time arrives you will tend to the concern. It empowers you to manage the difficulty, leading to increased personal control and a heart open to happiness.

This is a condensed but thorough list of journaling tools and what you can accomplish from each.

You might be thinking that journaling sounds great, but what if you died and all this cathartic, cleansing writing was discovered? What about all those mean things you wrote about your boss, your husband, Uncle Jerry or misbehaving children?

Just because I felt it, I would never want them to know it. That's fine. Your thoughts and impulses are your own private business. You are accountable for your behavior and your words.

I have many flowery journals. At first I just put things in code. If my husband and I had a three-day argument, it was translated in my account as a misunderstanding. I offered no clues of how it really was. It's okay to do that and still honor your feelings. You know how to decipher your code.

It's good practice to be prepared during a journal session. Have a packet of loose leaf paper or a roll of paper towels close at hand. When the emotion on the page gets rawer than the legacy you wish to leave, smoothly transition to the extra paper. You don't have to miss a beat. All of a sudden you're unedited. You get to use all the swear words your kids don't know you know. You can call names and fantasize about what you want to do. OOOOOHHH, that feels good!

When you get it all out, call in the burn pile or the trusty shredder, and erase it from existence. It's served its purpose. It's disposable. This editing tool can be used in any of the journal techniques if you want to keep your therapeutic nasties private. If you discover something worth preserving during these therapeutic rants, jot down a phrase or couple of words in your journal that helps you remember.

And that, my dear, is that.

Chapter 27:
Needs

As your self-knowledge increases, you'll begin to explore fulfilling your spiritual and social needs. While these are universal needs, the way you find fulfillment is your personal creation.

Spirituality is that inner path you take to discover the essence of your humanity, your life's meaning. However defined, it's part of your pilgrimage to happiness and connection to something larger than yourself.

Sometimes spiritual and social needs are met in the same place. Your path will likely bring you in contact with others on a similar journey, and you will find the community you seek.

Many find that a connection to a source of higher power provides grounding. Research indicates that belief in a power greater than oneself is a source of comfort. It's also been shown to enhance well-being and decrease stress. Studies show that personal and corporate prayer enhances health and healing. Seeking a spiritual path is a worthwhile quest.

Some find attending a place of worship is the best avenue, offering structure and community. Others prefer quiet and solitude as a spiritual base. Still others find their connection in nature.

Whatever path is right for you, you will discover a spiritual presence that will enhance your journey. This connection gives you an anchor, a sense of place. You never feel alone if you have that. You can draw on this connectedness for relaxation, meditation, and prayerful gratitude. It can help to sustain you during times of trouble.

We also need a connection to others. As social animals, we need each other. We yearn to feel loved and cared for. We need touch and emotional bonding. We need to belong.

At other times, we need to be alone. Some of us are extroverts. Others are introverts. Some are outgoing and engaging. Others are shy and socially anxious.

Are you an introvert or extrovert? The answer doesn't always lie in your level of sociability. What counts is how you rejuvenate. What do you need for fuel? The extrovert needs to be around people to get filled back up. The introvert needs time alone in the quiet. You can be social and still be an introvert.

Whichever it is, it's important to honor your need. If you start to feel worn out, edgy, and irritable, you might be running out of gas. It's important to know which type of fuel you use, high octane active or low octane solitude.

There is a wide spectrum of what constitutes a healthy social life. Some of us are more naturally sociable than others. They might still have friends from kindergarten and can make new friends at every social gathering. Others are shyer and most comfortable with a few close friends. At a party filled with strangers, they'll be the ones helping in the kitchen or studying the music playlists.

Turn your quest for a spiritual home and a social niche into an adventure. Attend different religious services. Attend a church, a synagogue, a mosque. Read books about world religions. Explore alternative expressions of faith. You will likely find that one visit stands out. There will be one place you feel at home. There may be some underlying emotional connection that you aren't immediately aware of, but follow the feeling.

A client of mine came from a background of several different Christian denominations, but she found the feeling of belonging in only one place. She loved the Catholic Mass. When she was attending other churches, her heart still yearned for the Mass. I encouraged her to return to the place that held her heart. Then we explored what it was about that service that gave her that sense of love and belonging.

It turned out that her grandmother was a Catholic convert who was fervent in her faith. Grandma had also been an angel of safety in her childhood, My client had childhood memories of attending Mass with her grandparents. The Christmas and Easter midnight services connected her to the glory and majesty of God. When there was a personal or national crisis, her grandma would take her to the church. Candles were lit in the darkness, and they would get on their knees and pray.

This was where she belonged. She might not have embraced the Roman doctrine, or even knew what all of it was. It didn't matter. God was there. The memory of her grandma praying, in her black lace head covering as her fingers gently caressed rosary beads, was where God lived for my client.

Whatever your social needs, some situations will take you out of your comfort zone, like work or social obligations. I also encourage you to seek other activities that take you out of your familiar space. Remember that a major part of growth is trying new things that are, initially, uncomfortable. Don't let fear hold you back from exploring. Seek out a new activity each day. It can be as small as walking down an unfamiliar street, or as momentous as attending a large civic activity like a prayer breakfast or a university seminar. You don't have to be a social butterfly to put yourself out there. You may feel tongue tied and anxious in some situations, but it will be okay. In the end you will be glad you pushed yourself. You might make new friends in the process, and gain a new hobby or passion.

Join pre-made social groups that spark your interest - church, school, running clubs, choruses, book clubs, and volunteer opportunities. Attend, smile, listen. Opportunities will arise to do other group activities like plays, dinners, potlucks, shopping trips, and sporting events. Speaking of sporting events, if you enjoy athletics, join city, park district, or health club sports teams. It's another great avenue for social engagement.

Chapter 28:
Peace

This section brings together much of what we've already discussed, and includes different tools and techniques to achieve stress management.

We've talked about using the breath to bring calm and lessen stress. Research shows that self-calming from breath work is valuable to manage anxiety and depression, stabilize blood pressure, increase energy levels, and relax muscles.

The most efficient method of getting full deep breaths is abdominal breathing. This is also called diaphragmatic breath because as you relax your abdominal muscles to inhale, you allow more space for the diaphragm to expand and create more room for the lungs. When the abdominal muscles contract on exhalation, the diaphragm also contracts to help the lungs empty.

Place your hand gently on your abdomen. You should feel it expand on inhalation and contract on exhalation. This gives a complete air exchange with each breath. Begin with cadenced "in-2-3-4 out-2-3-4" breathing to slow your respiration, reducing your body's stress signals.

This also brings your focus to the breath, which anchors you to the present moment. "Going to your breath" will become a catch-phrase when you start to feel tense or need to rejuvenate. It takes only a couple of minutes, but it can change your day.

There are many different breath patterns taught in yoga and other health practices. The breath is called pranayama in yoga. Prana means life force, reinforcing the physiological life force of breathing as well as the emotional and spiritual life force of the breath.

The following is a brief overview of relaxation and meditative practices. The breath is the entry point and focus in every technique.

Meditation: We looked at goals and challenges of a meditation practice earlier when we discussed mindfulness. Research confirming the positive benefits of meditation continues to amass. These benefits are wide-ranging, including emotional well-being and physical healing. Studies show changes in the brain's processing of stress with regular meditation.

There are many schools of practice, from Transcendental Meditation and Zen meditation to less formal but equally effective methods. Each focuses on coming to your center. You will find the same goal in most styles of meditation as well. I recommend no one over another. Research several methods. The relaxation state in each provides peace, calm, rejuvenation, and healing.

Your stage of life and availability of time are factors to consider as you select what's right for you. Be realistic. Avoid setting yourself up for failure. Again, it's the essence and quality of the practice more than the quantity.

Guided Imagery: This is a word picture that uses all the senses. It often includes a nature scene like a mountain stream, thunder and rain, or listening to birds. However, your mental happy place can be as simple as envisioning washing dishes, working in the garden, or taking a bubble bath. The only criteria are that you are able to create the image in your mind, and that being in the scene relaxes you.

The example I present is my own favorite place—the beach. The vastness of the sea and the rhythm of the waves feels primal. The synchronicity of the moon and the tides give me a sense of place in the universe.

Sit in a comfortable chair or lie down. Please, try this. See how it feels:

You're dressed in beach wear, carrying a beach towel and a book. A sandy path leads you to a wooden crossover. You climb the dunes on a worn, sand-gritty wooden walkway. At its peak, the brilliant blue ocean comes into view. You see it, but you can't hear it or smell it yet.

Stand there a minute and let the sea's infinity touch your heart. At the bottom of the crossover, your bare feet sink into soft sand. As you continue to walk you begin to hear the surf. The rhythm of the waves is the music of the sea. It sounds like God breathing. Smell the salt in the air mingled with tropical sunscreen and oranges.

Off with your flip flops! Your toes are enveloped in warm, damp sand as you move to the slowly lapping, low-tide waves that lazily massage your feet. As you stand at the water's edge, you feel the sand being pulled from under your toes as the waves return it to the sea. The gentle breeze wisps your hair around your face. Sanderlings skitter along the water's edge, chattering amongst themselves. You marvel at the crystalline blue water and the iridescent spray of the waves. Then you close your eyes and breathe slowly and evenly with abdominal breathing. Feel the sun's warmth on your bare arms. Taste the salt that hangs in the warm summer air. Stand there. Be present. Fully experience this moment, and the peace it brings. After a few minutes you will find your spot on the sand. Lie down on your beach towel and read a good book, nurtured and energized by your moment by the sea. Offer gratitude for the gift of the moment, and let the peace surround your soul.

Deep Muscle Relaxation: This form of relaxation also has guided direction, but the focus is more physical. It is a head to toe, muscle group by muscle group, full body relaxation. You can start from the head or the toes. Purposefully focus on each muscle group as you work your way up or down. Notice areas of your body that are holding more tension. Is your neck stiff or your abdominal muscles tight? Pay a bit more attention to these areas as your proceed.

Each muscle group is first tensed then let go, until your entire body is in a natural state of relaxation. Rest there for a bit, using abdominal breathing to maintain the relaxation. Again, scan your body, and notice if there are any spots that still feel tight. Go back to them, and focus there until your entire body is calm and peaceful.

Once you become adept at this, the process can be shortened by doing a whole body tensing and letting go. You can repeat this two to three times, then go to the breathing.

I taught my clients an even briefer version, tensing and releasing the hands. This is good for occasions when you feel anxious but don't have the opportunity for a full relaxation session. Clench both of your hands into fists, tensing all the way up your arms. Hold that tension for a minute as you take a deep breath in. Then quickly release your hands by flinging them open as you audibly exhale - *aaaahhhhh*. Energy will sizzle from your fingertips as the tension leaves. This is a helpful technique if you're preparing to give a presentation or about to go onstage. Standing in the wings, fling away those last-minute butterflies. Take a cleansing breath, put on a smile, and walk confidently to the stage.

Yoga: Yoga is another method of reducing stress, yet it can also be much more. The word "yoga" literally means to yoke or to join together. It has its roots in ancient India, and is a physical, mental and spiritual practice. The primary focus is to quiet and calm the mind. As our mind becomes more peaceful, we feel unified with our self and others and more aware of our place in the world.

For many Americans, the physical aspect of yoga has been seen as primary, but if you practice regularly, you'll also become aware of the mental and spiritual benefits. As you transition to higher-level practice, you'll find that even as you're engaging in challenging postures, you remain in meditation.

In stressing the spirituality of yoga practice, I don't mean to minimize the more material benefits. Yoga improves balance and flexibility. It also strengthens muscles, especially the core. The yoga asana (poses) stimulate the lymphatic system and massage internal organs, which improves blood flow and increases the strength of the immune system. There are asana for specific issues, such as sinus problems, sore throat, and headaches, to name a few.

Yoga is an excellent meditative practice. A yoga class begins with the breath or pranayama to quiet and center. The breath is used throughout the class during the different asana. The class will include poses that stretch, strengthen and improve balance.

A meditative time called shavasana, also known as corpse pose, ends a class. Each student lies on a mat in a manner that resembles a corpse, with individual variations. Your body is open and vulnerable. This quiet time provides the opportunity to re-center inward. It's brief, but follows the basic principles of meditation—focusing on the breath and letting thoughts pass through without catching hold.

You may be asked to join the class in an "Om" mantra at the beginning or end. The vibration of the Om breath is said to decrease stress signals in the body. It's called the sound of the universe—again, speaking of oneness.

At the conclusion of class it's traditional to honor the teacher by a slight bow and saying "Namaste," which honors the divine spark in each of us.

Yoga is for all ages and body types. It's also fine for folks with physical limitation. Poses can be modified to accommodate your capabilities, including chair yoga for people who have trouble getting up from the floor or standing.

Yoga isn't competitive. It is yours. Do what you can or want to do. You'll see changes in your body's power and flexibility as you continue. It's called a practice because it is said you never become an expert. You always have room for learning and growth.

I've practiced yoga since the early nineteen-seventies with some degree of regularity. It has accompanied me from my twenties to my sixties. My practice changes with age, but it will be a part of my life until I die.

It can be that way for you too. If you haven't tried yoga, please do. You can develop a home practice, but I recommend going to classes first to get the guidance of a good teacher in learning the proper forms of the asana. A class also becomes a community, as the group meditative experience brings you closer to one another. Once you know what your body feels like when it's in the proper alignment for a pose, it's easier to practice at home too. But I encourage committing to a regular class at least once a week, and more frequently if you can.

Tai Chi: This ancient Chinese practice was originally a form of self-defense. The full name is Tai Chi Chuan, which is literally translated as "supreme ultimate boxing". While considered a martial art, it also led to achieving a meditative state of mind. It has developed into more of a health practice to decrease stress and anxiety. The practice is comprised of a set of gentle flowing movements that bring relaxation and balance. I haven't learned Tai Chi so I can't personally vouch for it, but I know many who practice regularly and find it healing and rejuvenating, as well as providing a strong sense of self-control and mental discipline.

Massage: In most forms of de-stressing, you play an active role in reducing your stress and anxiety by using breath, exercise styles, and meditation. One plays a more passive role during a massage. You recline, and someone else relaxes your muscles. You can enhance the relaxation that results by focusing on your breath. Be fully present during your massage. Make a concerted effort not to think about your to-do list for the rest of the day or worry about a future challenge. With that open mind, as you begin to relax, massage becomes its own form of meditation.

There's a strong connection between muscle tension and the feelings we hold. Don't be concerned if during a massage tears spring to your eyes and emotions are released. This is another form of healing. You may find it helpful to journal after you finish a massage.

I advocate regular visits to a massage therapist. If you've never experienced relaxation that way, give it a try. Get a session scheduled. One hour is best. The therapist will talk with you before the massage to assess any trouble areas. She'll work those areas specifically along with a general massage.

Essential Oils and Aromatherapy: Essential oils have been used throughout history. In ancient times they were used medicinally. Today aromatherapy has become a common practice again. While no conclusive scientific studies support curative properties, there is strong anecdotal evidence of the healing properties of this practice. Many alternative therapeutic approaches to health advocate oils for any number of conditions.

If you're interested in this topic, get a book on essential oils. Their uses and combinations constitute a vast ocean of information. It's also important to deal with reputable companies for the purest, highest quality oils.

Try combinations to find what interests and pleases you. Personal experience will define how you choose to use essential oils. Maybe you'll limit your use to those that are personally pleasing and relaxing. Or you may also, after researching, use oils more extensively for emotional and physical health.

I use aromatherapy in my home, and I did in my practice. I'm particularly fond of lavender for relaxation and rest. Place a diffuser in a bedroom or special space. Mist the scent on clean sheets and on your pillow for restful sleep. I also have lavender plants growing near doors and windows. Rain brings out the fresh lovely smell. It's comforting and calming. I like peppermint and tangerine for energizing. For sinus issues eucalyptus in a diffuser is helpful. It's also good to tie a couple sprigs of eucalyptus to your shower head. It will naturally infuse your bathroom with a soothing aroma. You can do the same with lavender sprigs for relaxation.

Other: There are many other tools for relaxation out there, such as reflexology, herbal interventions, adult coloring books, labyrinths, and art or music therapy. All can be meditative, mindful experiences. Feel free to employ any you find useful, and have fun with your research!

Chapter 29:
Service

Depression, anxiety, defensiveness, fear, and mistrust have one thing in common. They're self-focused. There is a self-monitoring function in the hyper-vigilance needed to safely navigate a day. It's a protective mechanism–another one that often outstays its welcome. While it feels safe, it also makes us selfish and suspicious.

As you venture out of your comfort zone and try new skills, you'll see how self-centeredness can get in the way of embracing and appreciating the world. Once gratitude replaces defensiveness, anticipation replaces mistrust, and love replaces fear, the world becomes a different and far more welcoming place.

As you become more able to embrace the positive, you'll find happiness surrounds you. It's another step on that path to becoming an authentic, open, loving human being. With newly-opened eyes, you'll begin to see the needs of others more clearly.

The sleep deprived new mom next door, the retired couple across the street who rarely leave their house, the pre-teen down the road who comes home to an empty house after school? You'll notice, and be more inclined to help.

The clothing drive at church, the distribution of filled book bags at the community center, the reading to nursing home residents who stare into space from a wheelchair? You'll notice them too—and will be more inclined to help.

Once our eyes are opened, it's hard to return to being the protected, mistrustful, fearful person who peeked through the curtains but did nothing, who waited for others to answer the need of the less fortunate and forgotten souls. Or who didn't notice them at all.

In the process of transformation, your self-esteem, gratitude, and joy will increase. Your heart expands as you make a difference in the lives of others. Don't let this growth pass by without grasping it.

One of my clients lived a life filled with chronic anxiety and fear. Every once in a while he would casually mention an activity during the past week that had been out of his comfort zone. One week after a local natural disaster, he offhandedly reported he'd helped a friend search through the rubble of a destroyed house to find anything salvageable. Another time, he'd taken in neighbor children he barely knew for a weekend after their mother was hospitalized.

Each time one of these events occurred, I excitedly explored its significance. I reflected on his courage to step forward and respond spontaneously to another's need. But he couldn't give himself credit. He wouldn't own the growth. He retreated to peeking out from behind the curtain. He admitted he scared himself when he did these "risky" things.

But another client, a timid widow who'd never done anything without her husband, went with a friend to take meals to a homeless shelter once. She went back home to her secure, safe spot, but kept thinking of the women and children she'd met that day. So she went back again, pushing through her timidity. This time she stayed a bit longer to see if she could be of any help. She ended up reading to small children for two hours, and taking cookie orders to bring next time she came.

This one visit led to years of volunteering at the shelter, as well as at soup kitchens and food pantries. She went from a timid, dependent woman to a vibrant, active civic angel. On reflection, she now says she can't even remember what it was like to be anything else.

You don't have to change the world. But taking that first step can be eye-opening. Think about where you can take a gamble. Where do you want to freely give of yourself? Maybe it's as basic as picking up litter, or volunteering at a school across the street, or shelving at the library. The first steps are to get you out of the house and outside of yourself. From there, who knows where you will go or what you'll accomplish.

Once your eyes are open to the needs of others, your life adventures begin, and emotional freedom is yours.

Chapter 30:
Space

We've spent a lot of time on self-care and mindfulness. By now, it should be evident that you can practice these skills anywhere, anytime. Both gifts integrate into everything you do. But it's helpful to establish a refuge, a place that symbolizes the critical personal value of your practice.

This tool is designed to assist you in creating that space. This will be a spot in your home, yard, or neighborhood for quiet time. For the sake of illustration, I'll locate it at home. Maybe you have an extra room, a corner in your basement, or even a closet. It might just be a chair. It's the essence of your space that counts, not its size.

This is another one of those exercises that is self-affirming in itself. By creating this special space you show yourself you are worthy, and deserve to be treated in a loving manner.

***

Exercise 12: Design your sacred space, happy place, quiet chair, or comfort closet. Decorate it with special things that make you feel soft and peaceful, loved and happy. Candles and scents are nice, as well as flowers and plants or a small fountain. A favorite blanket or throw might feel cozy and nurturing. Add meditative music if you like. These are common elements for peaceful meditation, but don't lose sight of your unique needs. There may be a picture, a stone, a fragrance that has special significance. These personal additions are the most beneficial. They have a direct link to your heart.

This is to be your *space only. You'll feel a tendency to give it away or share it as soon as it's visited by your child with a question or husband with an important event to share. But keep the boundary firm. Make a sign to hang on the door or over the back of your chair that reads* Do Not Disturb *or* Meditation in Progress. *If it helps maintain the boundary, add* I love you, and I will be available soon. I look forward to spending time with you after my quiet time. *Your refuge is not to be violated by partners, children, mothers, or pets (unless you have a peaceful cat that sleeps at your feet). The space has to stay alive and vibrant in its tranquility and its "youness." For that, it needs to be loved and cared for, just like you.*

Now spend time there each day. You might have an hour to meditate and read. It may only be five precious minutes, or even just one. That's okay. As long as you close your eyes and breathe, it will become the sanctuary you need. It's the purposefulness of your attention to your own needs that makes this an irreplaceable time of rejuvenation and restoration.

Chapter 31:
Therapy

If reading these pages sparks a desire to spend time with a therapist, I encourage you to do so. Everyone should have the opportunity for counseling. It's a valuable tool in a quest for self-knowledge, and especially helpful when life challenges arise. I wish a year of counseling was required after college age. But I may be biased!

Here are some suggestions that may help, if you choose to embark on this adventure. The thought of making that first call can make your wring your hands, and the first visit may feel intimidating. Below are questions you might have about the process and their answers. I want to demystify counseling so you begin with enough information to minimize anticipatory anxiety.

I've used the terms therapist and counselor interchangeably throughout this volume. By this I mean counselors, social workers, and psychologists with licensed credentials. While there are differences, you can be comfortable and accomplish most therapy goals with any of them. The main distinction is in education requirements and treatment perspective.

How do you find a therapist? The first step is to ask others, just as you would when looking for a dentist or a contractor. You can also get a list from your insurance provider or your work employee assistance program. If you're insured, it's important to contact a therapist in your network to get your maximum coverage.

Have any trusted friends or family members been through a counseling experience or know someone who has? What about your pastor, advisor, mentor, or primary care physician? These are all good resources.

Once you have names, access the website of the therapist or the group he or she is affiliated with. Most counseling practices have pictures, credentials, specialties, and brief biographies of their staff. Check out how the person looks and what they have to say. One of my client's daughters selected a therapist from a picture, and because the biography stated she'd never met a book she didn't like. Some things just click.

Think about who you would feel most comfortable with. Take into consideration gender, age, specialty, and practical issues, such as ease of accessibility to their office and hours they are available for appointments.

Some of us relate better to men or women. Age preference might depend on your season of life. Many therapists specialize in certain age groups, such as children, adolescents, or young adults. Some treat only families and couples. Many older people prefer an older therapist. In the last few years of my practice, many elders came to me, mainly because they could tell by my picture and years of experience that I was over fifty.

Some therapists specialize in trauma, addictions, abuse, or grief. Some specialize in couples, sexual, or LGBTQ issues. If you know you have a specific problem or wound that holds you back, check if any counselors or therapists specialize in that area.

Their biographies often include information such as whether the therapist is married or has children. Some of us feel more comfortable with a therapist who has been through the trenches of parenthood or marriage. You may want someone who specializes in spiritual or religious counseling.

If you forgo the research and randomly pick a name from a local listing, you might still have a good fit. If you have the time, though, I recommend the longer route. Your journey and needs are important. Take time to honor that by doing your research. Send the message to yourself that you're worth the time.

Your relationship begins with your first call to the office. Ideally, the person who answers is warm, encouraging, and gives you a positive first impression. She will likely be able to set up your appointment and give you instructions regarding your initial visit. In some practices the counselors set up their own appointments. Don't be alarmed if you have to wait a few days!

When you enter the office on appointment day, you should find it warm and comfortable. You'll have paperwork to complete. This was likely explained in your initial phone contact. Arrive early enough to get it done before your appointment time. Your hour with the therapist begins then. Don't waste it. Generally, your therapist will escort you to his office at the time of your appointment.

I'd like to tell you waiting rooms are always a sea of tranquility. In reality, it depends on when you're there and the type of specialties. There's a more active dynamic if the practice has a heart for families and children. The presence of youth creates a different energy, similar to a house when children or teens are present.

Turn your phone off, or put the ringer on vibrate or silent. If you get a call you absolutely have to take, step outside. Don't be the disruptive person disrespectfully chatting away. Phone etiquette and manners provide mutual respect in a room where hearts are vulnerable.

What happens in the office with your therapist? It depends. Every counselor has certain goals in the first session or two. We're all unique in style, but a few generalities exist.

The paperwork you filled out needs to be reviewed. The therapist will elaborate and answer questions about policies. Your legally protected confidentiality, and its exceptions, must be discussed before you start sharing. Ideally, you're given an opportunity to ask questions you might have about the therapy and the therapist. The goals of the initial sessions will be explained.

The counselor might address your preference if you should run into each other outside the office—at the grocery store or community function. This is a confidential relationship. The therapist wants to be respectful of that should an encounter occur. Generally, acknowledging each other is left to the client to initiate.

After the routine information is done, the session generally proceeds to your chance to tell your story. The therapist will ask you routine screening questions and probably take a lot of notes. He or she may ask you to complete questionnaires or assessments that help clarify your situation.

Sometimes a client enters in acute distress—a recent death, a spouse abruptly leaving, or other traumatic event. In those crisis situations, the therapist will simply let the client talk and talk or cry and cry. The only goal then is to establish connection, listen, and engender hope. It's also important to assess whether this hurting soul with the wide open wound is safe and has the support to sustain him until the next session.

After the first session, you might feel as though it was a good experience and look forward to continuing. Or you may feel vulnerable and defensive, concerned that you shared too much with a stranger. I usually asked new clients to commit to four to six sessions. It often takes that long to know if this is a good fit and see if there's a therapeutic relationship building. That relationship will become the most effective tool of your work together.

On rare occasions, you might want to run out of the office because it was such a bad disconnect. Most therapists are good to excellent, but as in all professions, there are exceptions. That's one reason word of mouth is helpful. But remember, you are unique. The perfect therapist for your aunt's cousin may not be right for you.

Many counselors have a story that led them to the profession. A colleague once said we all start out trying to heal our own families. It's only after they realize they can't that they become professionals.

I can vouch for that. I look back and see I was a therapist at eight years old. I sat at the table with my parents, mediating and peacemaking through the latest argument. It was at that Formica kitchen table, cool to my elbows as I leaned into their storm, that I got the first inkling of being the one with good sense. It took me years to get all that sorted through, but going through my pain and honoring my own wounds made me a better therapist. There's a richness in having that experience, an increased respect for ourselves and the ones we lead through their own journeys.

Ideally, you will feel accepted, and sense your therapist is fully present and listening. One of the great paradoxes of the relationship is, if done right, it will be one of the most intimate connections you'll ever experience. At the same time there will be clearly defined boundaries. This is a professional helping relationship. If you were to become friends outside the office, the dynamic and effectiveness of this relationship would change.

That boundary is essential for both of you. A degree of self-disclosure by your counselor is a natural part of the relationship as you gain trust in each other. You'll learn bits of personal life, experiences, and taste. But you really don't want to know the nitty-gritty of your therapist's home life. You're there to talk about you.

I saw a therapist periodically over a span of twenty years. He always looked scholarly in three piece suits, graying hair and glasses. He never seemed to change though sometimes five years passed between visits. This was who he was for me. His office was warm and masculine. Multiple windows opened to a stand of woods. This was where he belonged. We had a deep connection, and he remains one of my most valued persons today. But I wanted him there, looking wise, in that space surrounded by his books, plants, and trees.

Once I saw him from a distance at a video store. It was a ninety plus degree July afternoon. His jacket and tie were off and his blue shirt collar open. He was perspiring and his hair was disheveled. He looked tired and worn out. I didn't approach him. We talked about it later, and made therapeutic use of the sighting. He had his place in my life, a sacred, safe niche, not to be violated by the outside world.

It's important that you be an active participant in your therapy. We don't yet have lab tests, x-rays, and scans of your heart and mind, but there will likely be more diagnostic tools available as the science of brain scanning progresses. But for now, there is no A-B-C written protocol for specific diagnoses. Your therapist relies on you for data to make assessments. Your ability to be honest and transparent is essential to get to mutually-agreed-on goals and treatment. You're not helping if you hold back or lie. You don't have to sugar-coat anything or try to please anyone in that office, though you may want to. It takes time to understand that the therapist is not going to judge or abandon you. You should experience unconditional positive regard, possibly for the first time.

Let your therapist know what you're feeling about the work the two of you are doing. Everything counts. If you come up with a plan together, don't sit there thinking *This won't work. I'll never do that,* while nodding agreement. Say "This plan is not going to work. I will never do that. We need to come up with something else." If you feel offended by something your therapist said, say so. Share.

Your relationship is a "life lab." The risks you take in this safe environment, you will eventually be able to take with an emotionally absent partner or a hyper-critical boss. If you leave a session with disappointment or anger, bring it back to the next session. If you don't, seeds of resentment will sprout, and you'll begin to behave the way you have in past broken relationships.

It's okay to speak up. We're not infallible! Don't be intimidated or reluctant to challenge a "professional." The fact is we all provide a service that you pay for, just like the person who takes care of your car. If your car continued to ping after a visit to the garage, you'd call the mechanic and let him or her know. Why would you treat your vehicle better than you do yourself?

My passion for the art and craft of therapy has never waned. I respect it and trust it. I hope I've illustrated enough nuts and bolts of getting started with a therapist. I want to remove the last remnants of fear and hesitation that might hold you back.

Over the years, I've assisted thousands of souls on this journey of healing to see happiness. The right therapist is out there waiting for you!

Chapter 32:
Time

Value the time spent working on your journey, but don't let the quest consume you. Some conscientious, responsible people tend to make any endeavor a full time job, including this one. Between therapies, self-help books, and support groups, you could actually miss the life you're trying to achieve.

Remember to make time for less serious forms of self-care like laughter and silliness. Take time to enjoy yourself and those you love. Take a break from the arduous labor of getting everything right. Laugh out loud and roll on the floor with the dogs. It supplies feel-good endorphins and creates mindful moments of bliss.

I often gave clients assignments to watch funny movies or sitcoms. I've prescribed a fun beach read, raucous detective mystery, or naughty romance novel. I've ordered a journal or support group ban some weeks, and encouraged a trip to the zoo or a nature center instead. Daily assignments have been suspended to experience an evening sunset or swans on a lake. These are all as healing as a therapy hour.

Don't take yourself too seriously! Learn to laugh at yourself and with others. It's liberating and enriching. Time away from your work can stir your unconscious so you return with a new perspective.

In the midst of life's stresses, you might not feel laughter in your belly. It can be a journey in itself to find where the giggle bubbles way down deep. Lighthearted laughter might feel like a forgotten joy, vaguely remembered from childhood. It's still there, maybe buried, but you can find it.

Some of us have to relearn laughter. You might have to prime it. A laughter yoga class might help you find your trigger. Some cancer centers and therapy clinics offer laughter groups. There's nothing like an infectious laugh spreading spontaneously. Check out *Most Contagious Laugh* on YouTube. You'll start out thinking how silly it is. You might mutter under your breath that it's a waste of your time. Stick with it. It's infectious. It's liberating. Sometimes that first awkward giggle can transport you to fits of guffaws. Learning this skill is mandatory for your journey. Let's go for the kind of giggles where you end up snorting stuff out your nose, crying, and fearing you'll wet your pants.

Kahlil Gibran told us in *The Prophet* that one cannot know great joy without experiencing sorrow. Just as laughter is important, tears are of equal value. Don't be afraid to cry. Whether the source be joy, sadness, or bittersweet memories, you need to let tears roll down your cheeks. Damming them up is as emotionally damaging as plaque blocking your arteries is physically. When you cry, you can feel emotions fall from your eyes. Stuff gets released and cleaned out like a spring rain cleansing the air of pollen.

We carry grief remnants that deserve to be honored by tears. One crisp October night when I was twenty-four, my dad died in an auto accident on a cornfield-lined country road. There are still occasions when a song, a smell, a memory will bring up the sadness. Thoughts of what he missed, what my children missed, crystallize in my heart and dissolve out my eyes. Never be ashamed that you still miss someone so many years later. It's a testament to the love and joy that person brought to your life.

Tears can also be a clue for future work. Have you ever sat in a theater watching a movie with friends? You hear a few sniffles as a sad scene unfolds. All of a sudden you're sobbing, great heaving hiccups of tears. Tissues are passed down the row as you continue to cry. Once you slow down, you realize you were the only one impacted so intensely by the scene.

There might be a reason your response is out of sync with that of others. What's being acted out on the screen has triggered an unconscious memory. What is discovered on exploration can lead to another level of healing.

A client received his first awareness of abandonment issues during such a movie. His mother's chronic "kidding" threats of leaving him damaged his sense of safety as a child. The emotions were unleashed as he watched a homeless woman leave her daughter swinging on a swing. Her child happily played on, unaware that a state worker was coming to take her away.

This movie mother wanted to give her daughter a better life. But what my client saw was the hysterical child being carried away screaming over the social worker's shoulder, "Mommy! Don't leave me! Mommy! Don't leave me!" He sobbed in the dark, feeling heart-wrenching grief and sorrow for the small girl on the screen—and the little boy who was himself. His inner child had always been afraid his mommy would leave, never to return. He shared his feelings with me and we worked it through. He achieved a new level of forgiveness for his wounded, childlike mother whose only desire had been that he cling to her always, even if it was out of fear.

I'm glad he was able to openly express his emotions. Men and women are wired differently. Women seem to have a chain of DNA that connects the heart and the eyes. Feel it . . . out it comes. Between that wiring difference and the software downloaded through culture and family, men often find it more difficult to cry. I've spent hours teaching hurting men that it's okay to cry out loud, sobbing tears. It's okay!

With each passing generation, though, men and women seem to come closer to emotional parity. Every passing of the torch leaves a bit less of the "Real men don't cry" and the "Shut up, or I'll give you something to cry about."

Take time. Feel your life fully, and express it authentically—both joy and sorrow. Don't work so hard all the time. Let the world and your friends provide healing along the way. As you follow this formula, shady glades filled with flowers will open along your path.

Chapter 33:
Words

Remember The Environmental Working Group's Dirty Dozen and Clean Fifteen foods? I've created a similar list of eight clean and dirty words and phrases, the nurturing versus the toxic. We've spent a lot of time on the stream of negative self-talk we administer to ourselves daily, and the positive self-talk we can use to combat this toxic habit. This tool makes it easier. There are certain words or phrases you should never utter to yourself. On the other hand, some words and phrases need to be delivered daily.

The Dastardly Dirty Eight:

1. *Should, shouldn't, ought.* This is a triple play of dirty words. Each implies judgment and encourages guilt. If you should or ought to do something, it means you don't want to but either an external pressure or internal self-talk tells you you're worthless if you don't. You're placing a value judgment on your decision. "Shouldn't" is punitive and guilt inducing.

2. *Stupid, dumb, dummy,* ___ (fill in blank). These are name calling—verbally abusive—words we mutter under our breath toward ourselves. You may have your own little list of nasties you use to slime your self-esteem. Come clean and add them to this dirty list. Just because you make a mistake or made an error of judgment, it does not equate to being stupid or dumb. You

made a mistake. So what! Learn from it and go on without judgment or self-recrimination.

3. *I never do anything right.* Never use "never," especially in proclaiming yourself a bumbling fool. If you never do anything right, you give yourself a pass from trying. You're done without ever getting in the game. Tell yourself to just "stop it."

4. *I can't do it.* These words are dream squashers, joy-killers, and excuse-makers. If you tell yourself you can't, it's a step backward from ever making the effort to try. Any attempt you make is half-hearted and ineffective. You've already charted the outcome, so why try? Your last words on the topic will be—"See, I told you I couldn't do it."

5. *Someday I'm going to. . :* This may not be the dirtiest of the dirty. For some it can be a part of a goal setting statement. If you use it in that constructive way, be sure to set a timeline for your goal, create a plan to achieve it, and note it on your vision board. The main reason this one makes the list is that it's my very own dirty word phrase. I tend to dream big and not follow through. Referring to writing this book, my wise daughter once said, "Mom, you always say 'someday.' When are you going to actually do it?" Now that the book is a reality, I get to add my own stinkin'-thinkin' to this list!

6. *I don't deserve it.* What have you ever done that leaves you undeserving of anything? You have a multitude of gifts given by grace, having nothing to do with what you deserve. Accept them with gratitude and enjoyment. You work hard for everything else. If you worked to accomplish a goal and won the prize, you deserve to celebrate. Accept the good feelings that come from perseverance and achievement. Appreciate the accolades. You *do* deserve it.

7. *I can't catch a break.* Sometimes this is true, but if you spend your life sitting back and passively waiting for your ship to come in, it's not going to. Work for what you want. The folks

you think have all the luck are the ones busy working to achieve their goals. You waste time waiting for luck to change. This is a form of self-pity. Self-pity sucks the life out of you.

8. *I don't want to get too excited. I may get disappointed.* Yes, this is another one of mine. Excitement and anticipation feel great, disappointment hurts. But why would you want to miss the good part because there's a chance you might end up sad for a bit? Excitement is a motivator. It keeps you going toward your goals, and supports a positive attitude. You cheat yourself when you hold back these feelings. Let yourself go. As motivational speaker Les Brown says, "Shoot for the moon. Even if you miss, you'll land among the stars." I interpret that as a signal to get excited and go for it. Even if what you hope for doesn't come through, you'll travel to uncharted places.

The Classy Cleansing Eight:

1. *You're lookin' good, Good Lookin'.* Do you ever say that to yourself? If not, time to start. Look in the mirror and tell yourself you're beautiful. Wink, smile, and say "You're lookin' good, Good Lookin." Do it in the morning before you've combed your hair or brushed your teeth, before coffee even.

2. *You can do it.* We often wait for others to encourage us. Become your own cheering section! Your own words have the most impact. Remember, you are your number one fan.

3. *You are worthy.* We often tell ourselves the opposite. This conveys a softness, a gentleness toward yourself. It's a reverent statement.

4. *I may be afraid, but I'll still try.* Don't tell yourself not to be afraid. Fear is a natural response to moving out of your comfort zone. Courage is not the absence of fear. It is pushing on in the face of trepidation. Don't let the scary stuff stop you. If you wait until you're not afraid, the time will never come.

5. *I love you.* Some of us never heard this as children. It's important to say these healing, affirming words to yourself.

Often. This is done best face-to-face in the mirror. Say it like you mean it, as though you're telling your child within who so missed hearing those words.

6. *My dreams can come true.* Also a phrase you might not have heard often growing up. It might be an alien concept. Push through your initial skepticism. Use that positive self-talk to slowly move to the positive. It's a dream come true in itself when you can believe these words.

7. *Things will get better.* Sometimes in the midst of sadness or fear, it's important to reassure yourself that this trial, challenge, or sorrow is temporary and will pass.

8. *My feelings are okay.* Earlier we discussed the value of validating feelings. It takes a lot of practice for this to become a core belief. Acknowledge your feelings without judgment. Keep what you want, and directly communicate those you want to share. Don't wait for someone else to give you permission to express what you feel.

Take a few minutes to add some personal words of affirmation to the list that challenge your own set of negative messages. We all have our own windmills to battle. I'm sure there are some ugly things you regularly say to yourself. Put them down with the other dirties. Also add good words that are helpful. If you can't think of any, then write down positive responses to your own personal bad word list.

As you know by now, the good word list is the one to use, practice, and incorporate in your life. It's the healthy, non-toxic food you need to nourish your soul.

Repeat the clean word list regularly. Also write down your encouraging, nurturing words on Post-it notes. Put them on your bedside table, bathroom mirror, coffee pot, computer, and car steering wheel. Record them on your cell phone if you can, then play it back when you need to hear kind words. Get a coffee or tea mug emblazoned with some blatant, sentimental self-love phrase. This will all seem unnatural at first. Remember, the only way something becomes a part of your comfort zone is by practice. So practice, practice, practice! Do not let the bad words come out of your mouth!

When you write down your personal list of dirty words, make the letters foreboding and malevolent, like dark shadows and haunted trees. If you catch a negative phrase falling from your tongue, immediately rinse your mouth out, literally or figuratively, as if you've tasted spoiled milk. Say "yuck" or some such word. Then wipe your mouth with the back of your hand. Take a deep breath and immediately tell yourself something lovely.

One thing you are absolutely NOT to do is berate yourself for a slip. Give grace. Be gentle. Give it a try. Keep practicing. After a time, you'll see a difference in how you treat yourself.

Part III

Chapter 34:
Your Legacy

During life's journey, do you ever stop and wonder what legacy you'll leave when you depart? I'm not speaking of a material gift or bequest. This is not about wealth, presents, or other physical markers or awards. What will others remember? What mark will you leave on the world? What stories of your life will future generations share with the next?

When we're young, we often think of this topic in terms of greatness. Will we find the cure for cancer? Build great buildings? Maybe be a great athlete, or a devout spiritual leader? I was going to be a great poet and novelist, my words quoted for generations to come, with maybe a Nobel Prize for literature along the way. We each tend to think in terms of our impact on the world, doing what we define as great works.

As we get older, though, our circle gets smaller. Rather than the world, we think of our family, our neighbors. We begin to understand that in order to improve the world, it has to be done one person at a time. To leave it a better place, we have to care for family, our friends, and people on our block. If we each focus on our small sphere of influence, then put it all together, it really can become a better world.

One of my elderly friends spent her life as a housewife and mother to five children, then grandma to multitudes of grandchildren and great-grandchildren—who all still came home for Sunday dinner. She was active in her church and the charities it sponsored. Her scope of influence was an approximately twenty-five square mile area.

When she fell ill with terminal cancer, she wondered at all the people who came to visit, who sent gifts, cards, and prayers. She said she couldn't understand it. She'd lived such an ordinary life. But the reality was, she'd lived an *extraordinary* life. She had quietly cared for others, freely giving of herself to family, neighbors, and church family. She was kind, honest, generous, and humble.

When February came, and she was nearing her time to leave this earth, my young daughter and I took her flowers and a Valentine my daughter had made. In all that was going on in her life, she took the time to write a thank-you note to my daughter. That thoughtfulness was such a natural part of her that she never thought twice about making the effort. My daughter still remembers that act. It became a part of this dear lady's legacy, carried on in a little girl's heart.

My own grandmother's life was also a legacy, to myself and others. She set an example for others by her service, loyalty, and dedication. In her later years, she was ravaged by a disease that eventually took her. By then, I was old enough to appreciate who she was as a woman—not just as my grandma. I saw her continue to do her job as a small-town newspaper editor as long as she could, and keep her promises to the community she loved. But most of all, I remember a grandmother who cherished her great-grandchildren, still toddlers at the time. She leaned on Grandpa to walk, but when the "babies" arrived, the orders were to help her get down on the floor to play. And play she did—trucks, Legos, blocks, Candyland. Whatever her great-grandchildren wanted her to do, she did. The assistance to get her back on her feet caused her pain, but her smile was joyful and without regret.

When I look back over my life, those who remain in my heart were people like my friend and my grandmother. They lived by example, and did the best they could with what they had been given. It wasn't the flashy actions or the grand schemes for greatness that impressed. It wasn't wealth or power that I remember. It wasn't those who talked so much about their good deeds. It was the simple lives of the honorable folks who did their best.

Maybe there should be a vision board for our legacy. This could include the kindnesses we want to remember to act on, the things we want to teach our children and our grandchildren, the spiritual gifts we want to leave. It would represent how we want to be remembered.

If this sounds like a good idea, incorporate it into your life goals. I've added it to my list!

Chapter 35:
Moving Forward

Over my thirty years as a therapist, I've changed as my life has changed. When I began, as a single nurse, I constantly got overinvolved. Following emotional fatigue and a couple years of therapy, I learned more effective boundary setting. At first, the pendulum swung to boundaries that were so fierce I rarely felt close to my clients. I did the work I was gifted to do, but stayed emotionally detached.

After I married and had children, I found a better balance for my time and energy, but still often felt burned out. During periods of emotional fatigue, I fantasized about being a sales clerk at a local department store.

I'm glad I stayed with my practice. Looking back, I see how my life crises and experiences took me deeper as a therapist. Arguments with my spouse, challenges with teenagers, trouble with in-laws, and caring for aging family members all made me a better problem solver and created a more empathic heart.

When our son Matthew was stillborn at thirty-five weeks, and when my mother became ill and died after months of caring for her, I was taken to deeper intimacy. Laid bare, I learned more about being vulnerable, even while respecting professional boundaries, as I processed my clients' feelings about personal tragedies and grief.

Over these years, children grown and marriage mellowed, I have come to a profound understanding of how much I've loved my work. My husband and I once coined the term "shadow-friends." His were a collection of coffee shop patrons, thrift shop volunteers, and neighbors he chatted with on the front porch. My clients, whom I had known for years, were among my "shadow friend" tribe. Except for the clinical boundary that made our work possible, they would have met the criteria of dear friends. What is a friend after all if not someone you can laugh and cry with, be there for, in their darkest moments, and love them for who they are?

Yes, there were times over the years that I disliked my job. There were days my calling drained me, and I came home empty. I was ready to quit on those nights. I picked up the wine glass and went to my room. Those nights I had no words for family and no heart to listen to them talk about their days. I couldn't take the risk in my rawness. I had to hide.

Sometimes I felt like an ancient sin-eater as I ingested confessions of fathers seeking absolution for their darkness. Other days I felt like John Coffey, the death row character in the movie *The Green Mile*, who breathed in others' illness and pain—healing them as he slowly weakened. I thought of him after days of bearing sorrow of grieving parents and holding hands of the lost and dying. Over thirty years, these times gathered in a corner of my soul. They hold a place of respect and reverence in my heart.

But the majority of my time was spent teaching, listening, guiding, and mediating. Sometimes I found this process challenging. At other times it all seemed simple, and we would celebrate by pushing the Staples *That was easy* button on my desk. These were rewarding days, acting as the emotional tour guide, problem solver, and goal maker.

I respect and honor the hearts that traveled their paths through dark scary spaces. These were journeys of great courage. I learned so much from my clients. I will always be nurtured and humbled by their trust and regard.

Chapter 36:
Saying Good-Bye

N ow I return to the memory of that last day in my office, shuffling through the basket of notes and cards.

I come across one from a couple who struggled with infertility. It contains a picture of their new baby boy, adopted only a few days before the picture was taken. A year later they adopted his newborn sister. Another card is a wedding invitation from a single woman who once believed herself to be unlovable, too tarnished by her father's hands to ever marry. It was a lovely wedding. I smiled at thoughts of the weddings, christenings, and funerals I attended. Tears trickle down my cheeks once more.

I hope you've found my accounting of this journey helpful. It was good to write it down and pass it on. It's gratifying to lay it out in a manner that may help others.

I'll leave you by revisiting some messages that I think are worthy of emphasis.

The first words that come to mind are personal control and choice. By embracing the child you were and learning who you are today, you are set free from the old bonds that hold you back from happiness. In doing so, you open yourself to the freedom of choice in your life, and learn to appreciate its power.

Remember, as an adult you no longer have to follow childhood rules. You have control. You have choice. Sometimes, the choice may only be in how you breathe and where you place your gaze. But you always have a choice.

I recently saw an inspirational quote from an unknown author. It reads, *A comfort zone is a beautiful place, but nothing ever grows there.* Don't shrink from the fear and discomfort that comes with leaving the familiar behind. It's only by moving out of your safe place that you add new growth — and create new places of comfort.

Remember that you are unique and precious. You deserve to be cared for. Practice saying good words to yourself, and quiet those negative voices of youth. Say, "Stop it" when they clamor to be heard. Don't forget that your own kind words are the most affirming. Use them generously. Give grace freely. Be nurturing and honoring in your self-care. Value the essence of time spent — quality over quantity.

Take time to laugh and love. Keep all your senses open to happiness, and snatch it up as it flirts with you. See the good in all. Be fully present. Live each day as if it's a precious gift, because it is. As Warren Zevon wisely suggested, "Enjoy every sandwich."

Share the gift with others, and be open to what others teach you. Find your niche — your place in the world and your relation to others. Keep your eyes open. Notice. Be a part of this lovely, messy, quirky, wise human tribe.

Respect your learning curve, and persevere. Don't let obstacles or setbacks defeat you. While I was writing these words, a memory of my son's junior high scavenger hunt came to mind. Several teams set out to find everything on their lists. Most returned without completing the task. My son's team was late returning, but as they walked back to the yard, the five of them slowly lugged a couch — the last item on the list. Others had deemed it impossible and given up. His group found a way.

You will find a way too. Be true to yourself and your goals. You too will accomplish what seems most challenging. Don't let fear hold you back.

For now, I leave you these gifts of understanding and knowledge. You now have a skill-filled toolbox for your journey. Use it as needed along the way. May you find contentment that comes from a life of meaning and substance. Open your heart to authentic relationships that bring you joy. I hope you and happiness meet at every turn, and the sparks build a lasting fire of peace in your heart.

I used to laugh and say, "I could do this work until I'm ninety. As long as I can sit up, nod, and not have drool on my chin, I'll be fine." That's not funny anymore. I honored my clients by leaving them while at my best. I would never disrespect them, or the work we did, by being less than fully present.

Now I sit back in that faded, old chair, holding treasured notes in my lap. I sit up straight, nod, and check my chin for drool. I gaze around the office one last time. My storage boxes are filled. The shadows are growing long.

It's time to go home.

End Notes

1. Ralph Waldo Emerson, *The Conduct of Life*, (1860), quoted in H. Jackson Brown Jr., *Life's Instructions for Wisdom, Success, and Happiness*. Nashville: Rutledge Hill Press: a division of Thomas Nelson, 2000.

2. Shel Silverstein, *A Light in the Attic*, New York: Harper Collins, 1974, p.139.

3. Marianne Williamson, *A Return to Love*, Harper Collins, 1992, pp. 190-91.

4. Margery Williams Bianco, *Velveteen Rabbit*, The Classic Edition, Kennebunkport: Cider Mill Press, 2013, pp. 8-11.

5. *Psychology Today*, Basics, "What is Mindfulness," 2017. https://psychologytoday.com/basics/mindfulness.

6. Ann Voskamp, *One Thousand Gifts: A Dare to Live Fully Right Where You Are*, Nashville, Harper Collins, 2011.

7. Jessica Cassity, "The Power of Mindfulness: Reshape Your Brain for Calm and Compassion." https://www.my.happify.com.

8. Ann Frank, *Diary of a Young Girl*, New York: Doubleday, 1947, p. 208.

Acknowledgments

Many people contributed to this book becoming a reality. First, I want to thank those who encouraged my writing, offered professional wisdom, and acted as guides in my own journey of self-discovery. Without them, it would have not been written.

Thanks to my sons and daughter and daughters-in-law for cheering me on, and my grandchildren for bringing joy. A special thanks to Jesse for his unwavering faith, Nick for his encouragement and editing, and Savannah for letting me know it was time to write this. My husband Marty was my first reader. He also got to be the one to talk me through my fear every time I was sure I couldn't do it.

Thanks to David Poyer and Lenore Hart, my publishers at Northampton House Press, for patiently walking me through my plodding work, and Frank Green for his close proofreading.

I also want to acknowledge Tony Morris and the other writers at the Ossabaw Island Writer's Retreat, Ossabaw Island, Georgia. This first step toward my post-retirement writing career left me humbled but inspired.

Most importantly, I thank my clients. Their courage, perseverance, and commitment taught me more than I could ever have learned from a textbook or college. Every day they inspired me with the power and resilience of the human spirit. I'm so thankful I could be a part of their journeys.

Northampton House Press

Established in 2011, Northampton House Press publishes selected fiction, nonfiction, memoir, and poetry. Check out our list at www.northampton-house.com, and Like us on Facebook— "Northampton House Press"—as we showcase more innovative works from brilliant new talents.

Made in the USA
Lexington, KY
21 May 2018